The Count Who Wished He Were A Peasant

A Life of Leo Tolstoy

Tolstoy was one of the most remarkable of all men, one of the great shapers of the world we live in.

As an artist—one of the world's greatest writers—and as a philosopher, Tolstoy tried to express his understanding of the meaning and value of life in universal terms, yet he himself was very much the product of one nation at a particular period in its development. The character of 19th century Russia into which he was born had two determining features: it was a political dictatorship and a slave society. During his lifetime, serfdom was abolished, although the government had not become any less oppressive, but the even more significant changes—the means for making individual life more valuable—for which Tolstoy had fought so hard, had yet to be fully realized.

Tolstoy was born a member of the land-owning nobility, yet he dedicated his genius to a crusade against inequality, slavery, and immorality of all kinds—social, political and economic.

Morris Philipson has drawn a complete and colorful picture of the great writer, philosopher and religious leader, of his childhood and youth, of his middle years and old age, of princes and peasants, of family and friends—against a vast panorama of a civilization in turmoil.

The Count Who Wished He Were A Peasant

A Life of Leo Tolstoy

by Morris Philipson

ILLUSTRATED WITH PHOTOGRAPHS

Pantheon Books

For Ernest J. Simmons

"The aim of an artist, {Tolstoy} once said, is not to resolve a question irrefutably, but to compel one to love life in all its manifestations."

—From INTRODUCTION TO RUSSIAN REALISM

Frontispiece photograph of Leo Tolstoy. Courtesy of The New York Public Library, Picture Collection

FIRST PRINTING

Contents

The Count Who Wished He Were A Peasant

A Life of Leo Tolstoy

Introduction

The Shape of Russian History

Though he came to be a man whose concern for humanity knew no limits of space or time, Leo Tolstoy was at first very much the product of one particular nation and culture, in a particular epoch of its development. He was an heir to Russian history — which contributed to the formation of his character under the special conditions of wealth, aristocracy, and privilege, for he was born a member of the land-owning nobility. Tolstoy grew to be a literary artist, an original thinker, and a moral force of world-wide significance, but his life began as exclusively Russian.

The estate of a great Russian landowner, until the middle of the nineteenth century, was more like property held by a medieval feudal lord than it was like anything else that existed in the rest of the world. It was an independent community able to supply all the needs of its master. The peasants worked the soil, planted and harvested the food, made the tools, the carts, the sleighs, and took care of the animals as they had for nearly a thousand years. Their wives spun the flax into linen, wove the wool and made the clothes, cooked and cleaned, and cared for the children. The master of such an estate might keep a priest in residence as he would keep a doctor, a tutor, an overseer for his farms, or musicians for entertainment. He recognized the political authority of the Czar's appointed governor over the province in which his lands were located, but on the estate itself he was the undisputed lord and master. He was the independent ruler of all he commanded, just as the Czar was the absolute ruler of the entire Russian empire.

From the point of view of England or France, in the early nineteenth century Russia was as backward socially, politically, and economically as the rest of Europe had been a hundred years before. But then Russia had followed a course of development very different from that of the rest of Europe.

In the days when Russia was first ruled by the descendants of Rurik the Great, the Viking warrior who founded a dynasty that lasted from 862 to 1598, the nation was a loose association of independent principalities. Each reigning prince was supported by his nobles, the *Boyars,* and by his knights and soldiers of fortune. The peasants ceased to live like savages in the forests and fields and became masters of the land they farmed; in the towns, artisans cultivated trades, and merchants thrived. A primitive form of democratic assembly developed — somewhat like the original New England town meeting. Cities expanded; prosperous Kiev was larger than London or Paris in the eleventh century. But all of that was to change.

The feudal princes had great political power. Free to support the dynastic ruler or not to, the independent princes fought each other more readily than they fought together against foreign enemies. Because of the disunity of the nobility and the superior military forces of the invader, Russia was conquered by the Mongols and made subservient, directly or indirectly, to the descendants of Genghis Khan from 1223 to 1480. This was the turning point in Russian history; these two and a half centuries made the Russians accustomed to Oriental despotism.

In 1462, when Ivan III came to power, he was determined to create a unified nation in order to free Russia of the Mongols. He fulfilled his purpose — but at the price of destroying both democratic forms among the peasants and the political independence of the nobles. Precisely at the time when many of Europe's lords and kings were gradually making it possible for more democratic rule to evolve, the Russians moved in the opposite direction toward despotic dictatorship. The ruler of Russia, who now for the first time called himself "Czar" (after the Roman "Caesar"), claimed all the powers to

Peter I, "the Great," Czar of Russia (1682-1725).

govern. The phrase "Autocrat of all the Russians" as part of the Czar's title meant that he alone was absolute ruler. Thus, in every important sense, by the end of the sixteenth century the nobles as a class no longer had any political influence whatsoever.

The next most significant transformation came about during the long reign of Peter the Great (1682-1725). It was his ambition to bring Russia out of her backwardness and make her a match for the rest of Europe. But he focused only on Europe's technology and industry without trying to adopt its political and social structure. He considered himself a servant of the State, and every man within his realm his co-worker. By his imperial order, the nobility had to serve in the army, navy, or civil government for twenty-five years or more. If they refused, the nobles were deprived of their estates and might be condemned to death. Forced to leave their homes for long periods of time, with their estates thus falling into decay or becoming impoverished by dishonest overseers, the nobles argued that the system undermined its own foundations. If it continued the nobility would disappear.

After Peter's death, the Imperial demands were relaxed. Catherine the Great (1762–96) tried to make up for the excessive obligations with new rights and privileges. She allowed the nobles to meet in provincial assemblies which had the appearance of parliamentary forms of government, but without ceding any of her political power. It was during the rule of this German-born princess that Russia moved even further toward dictator-ship — and at exactly the time that the American colon-ists, with the Declaration of Independence, undertook to create a new form of democracy based on equality. It is true that there were slaves in the United States. They were oppressed people brought to the land from a conti-nent different from that of the colonists; their language, color, and religion set them apart as a totally different breed. But Russia's slaves — its serfs — were Russians of exactly the same breed as their masters; and it was through Catherine's power that the stages by which they were enslaved reached their climax.

At the beginnings of Russian history the people who worked the land were of three types: *slaves,* meaning those who had been conquered in war or bankrupted freemen who sold themselves into bondage; *free migrant agricultural workers,* who moved about whenever they had to look for a new job; and *peasants,* the small farm-ers who worked their own land and were members of an independent rural community called a Commune. If such peasants settled on the land of estate-owners, monastaries, or the State, they paid a yearly rent in money, goods, or by working part of the time for masters of the land. But under Catherine the Great all three groups of workers were merged into the one class of *serfs,* who became the legal property of the landowners, the Church, or the State.

This profound change had come about gradually, over

Catherine II, "the Great," Empress of Russia (1762-1796). Painting by Lampe.

the course of centuries, in the following way. Land without agricultural workers on it is of little value to a landowner. A regular income from land depends on a stable number of people continuing to farm it. Therefore, landowners used all sorts of devices to hold their workers. The most unscrupulous of them kidnapped the peasants from the lands of weaker neighbors. Later a free peasant could not leave a particular estate until he had found someone to replace him. A peasant who settled on some proprietor's land rarely had enough tools, cattle, or money to keep his family going until the first harvest. He borrowed from the landlord, and the difficulty of paying back that original loan was usually enough to keep him from moving away. When the Imperial rulers demanded the services of the nobles and were unable to pay them with money, they rewarded them with grants of land along with a certain number of serfs *who did not have the right to leave the property.* Some of the peasants who were to work part of the time for the landowner became full-time servants in the master's house rather than laborers in the fields. But for hundreds of years it had been possible for a serf — even after he had lost the right to move away — to express his grievances against an unfair master through legal means by appealing to the local civil authorities. Eventually even that last protection was lost.

Without clearly defined laws governing obligations that went along with their privileges, the masters of estates exercised the same powers over their serfs as they did over their slaves. At its worst this means they treated them as private property; they bought them and sold them like cattle. The government received money as taxes on every sale of this sort and therefore willingly overlooked the fact that such sales were illegal. In 1767, by an edict of Catherine the Great, this transaction was made legal. For all practical purposes, serfs were slaves. From then on, a man's wealth was not calculated by how much money or land he controlled but — as the Russians put it — by how many "souls" he owned.

The shape that Russian history took, and the world that Leo Tolstoy inherited, had two overwhelming features: it was *a political dictatorship* and it was *a slave society*. At the time of Tolstoy's birth the population of Russia was approximately sixty million people. Fifty million of them were enslaved serfs.

Throughout his lifetime Tolstoy endured the unchanged oppression of being a "citizen" of a country in which no man had any political power except the Czar himself. During his lifetime serfdom was abolished, but he was then thirty-three years old, and, in any case, the conditions under which the serfs were "freed" did not bring about the improvements that he had hoped for. What matters most for understanding Tolstoy's life is the persistent truth that, as an heir to Russian history, he was brought up under the conditions of political despotism but with all the benefits and privileges of a landowner in a slave society.

He inherited an estate like that of a medieval feudal lord, "a world in itself." Perhaps partly because of being master of such a world he fearlessly became master of his own mind. Knowing both what it is to be master of a slave-supported economic world and the victim of a despotic political world, he came to argue, more effectively than anyone else in the world during much of his long lifetime, for the elimination of slavery in all forms of human relations.

I

Childhood

The first Tolstoy recorded in Russian history is said to have come to the land in 1353, a nobleman with a following of three thousand attendants. The family was probably of Lithuanian origin, they embraced the Russian Orthodox faith, and they were made members of the Russian nobility — hereditary counts — by the Grand Duke of Moscow two generations later. Peter Tolstoy (1645-1729) was a favorite of Czar Peter the Great. His great-grandson became governor of Kazan early in the nineteenth century, and the governor's son, Nikolai, fought against Napoleon in 1812. Ten years later Nikolai married Princess Marya Volkonsky, herself the descendant of one of the most aristocratic families in Russian history; she could trace her ancestry back to Rurik the Great.

Leo Tolstoy, the fourth son of Nikolai and Marya, was born on August 28, 1828. His parents had one more child, a daughter, when Leo was two years old, but, in the same year, his mother died. She had been a pious, warm-hearted, and well-educated woman. The estate she had inherited from her ancestors was her children's birthplace, and it was here that Leo was to live most of his long, fruitful, and extraordinary life. Russian history made up the public world he inherited; life on the wealthy estate where he was reared made up his private world.

The estate was called *Yasnaya Polyana,* which means a glade, a clearing in the woods, or clear meadow. It was located 130 miles south of Moscow, near the city of Tula. Two great whitewashed brick towers shaped like mushrooms with lacquered roofs stood at the entrance to the grounds. A road lined by birch trees ran from the gateway to the flower gardens in front of the mansion. Beyond it lay a park with ancient lime trees, ponds, stables, tennis court, and lawns. At the edge of the estate was the Zakaz woods and the Voronka river, where the family went swimming. The manor house itself, stately and handsome, with various wings and porches, numbered forty-two rooms and nearly as many domestic servants: butlers and valets, nurses, maids, cooks. It was a house full of life: a large family of relatives both close and distant who lived together and were visited often by friends and relatives who stayed for long periods of time. The sense in which it was "a world in itself" is beautifully

View of the Tolstoy country estate, Yasnaya Polyana.

and most clearly expressed by Tolstoy in his first published work, *Childhood,* where, in describing the feelings
of the eleven-year-old hero during the hunt one afternoon,
he says:

> The limitless, brilliantly yellow field was bounded
> only on one side by the tall, bluish forest, which
> then seemed to me a most distant, mysterious place
> beyond which either the world came to an end or
> uninhabited countries began.

In this private world Tolstoy lived his gilded youth.
His father was somewhat withdrawn from the company
of neighboring landowners; his personality was marked
by a certain sadness. He had served the Czar as an officer
and survived Napoleon's invasion, but he was disen-
chanted with social and political life just as he was with
military life. He had not achieved a brilliant career for
himself, but rather had made a "marriage of convenience" with a good woman of great wealth. Theirs was
no passionate love-match, but it was the conventionally re-
spectable thing for a man in his position to do. The
Princess and he had been good companions and enor-
mously devoted to their children. After her death, he became even more reserved. He lived the life of a nobleman
given to overseeing his lands, hunting, and reading, somehow detached by his dignity, worldliness, and charm.
Tolstoy's mother had been a person of greater intellect
and spirituality. While nothing could compensate for the
loss of her unique presence, there were many women in

the household who assumed the responsibility of rais-
ing the children after Marya's death.

First, there was Grandmother Tolstoy, widow of the
governor of Kazan, and her daughter, Leo's Aunt Alexandra, and Alexandra's ward, Pashenka. Alexandra had survived the gruesome misfortunes of marriage to a Baltic
count who went mad and tried to kill her. She had lost
her own child at birth and was given the baby of one of
her servants — Pashenka, whom she brought with her to
live in her brother's house. She was a devout Christian to
whom numerous monks and nuns and other religious
people made visits at Yasnaya Polyana. But the one who
was to have the most influence on Leo's childhood was
"Auntie" Tatyana, so called although she was no more
closely related than his father's second cousin. As an or-
phan, she had been brought up by Tolstoy's grandmother.
In her youth she had been in love with Nikolai, but (six
years after Marya's death) when Leo's father asked Tatyana to marry him and take care of his children, she accepted only the second half of the proposal. Truly she
became Leo's second mother. In his later years, Tolstoy
recalled her as the one who "by her whole being filled
me with love. I saw and felt how she enjoyed loving, and
I understood the joy of love. That was the first thing. And
the second was that she taught me the charm of an un-
hurried, tranquil life."

The earliest years of such a life were spent upstairs in
the nursery with his younger sister, in the atmosphere of

maternal care. Leo's three older brothers occupied rooms downstairs, with their German tutor. When it was time for him to leave cribs and nurses he took his place there among the older boys, where there was a promise of the world into which they would grow — the realm of his father, with its horses and dogs, the studies of the classroom, the companionship of men. As he described it years later, the move "downstairs" meant that "for the first time I felt that life was not a game but a serious matter."

Still, the forms of it followed the leisurely natural order of the rural life — the pleasures and the sports of exploring nature in all seasons and the ceremonious life of family celebrations, name-days, and holidays. Most important of all, even beyond the great comfort of his existence, was his good fortune in finding his three older brothers kindly and intelligent, thoughtful and imaginative. Dmitri, a year and a half older than Leo, offered boundless gaiety and merriment. Sergei, two and a half years older, handsome and self-confident, clever and mysterious, was Leo's first object of "hero worship." But it was Nikolai, nearly six years older, whose unusual qualities had the most long-lasting effect on Leo. Nikolai was a born leader and had, like their mother, a highly moral and altruistic nature. It was he who supplied Leo with what amounted to his special *manna.*

Nikolai made up folk tales and ghost stories, but he also read religious tracts and thought about moral problems. It was he who told his brothers one day that he knew a wonderful secret. Huddled together on the floor, in a hut made by covering chairs with a blanket, Nikolai revealed to his brothers that he knew what would make all men happy. He said he had written this secret on a green stick and buried it near the road at the edge of a ravine in the Zakaz forest. When the secret was known it would bring about a Golden Age for man on earth: there no longer would be disease or misery of any kind, and all human beings would become everlastingly happy. Nikolai stipulated conditions that were to last for a year. If his brothers fulfilled the requirements, the secret would be disclosed to them. The game was soon forgotten, but the effect on Leo was never lost.

Manna, the food supplied from heaven to the Hebrews wandering in the desert between Egypt and Israel, has come to symbolize spiritual nourishment. The childhood ideal of what the Green Stick would reveal functioned as an inexhaustible source of nourishment for Tolstoy's spirit. The hope that "understanding the secret" would enable man to eliminate evil and to live in happiness was the hope that never deserted him. Nikolai told the story of the Green Stick when Leo was a child. As a man of eighty, expressing his wishes for how and where he should be buried, Count Tolstoy requested that his grave be dug at the site of the Green Stick. It is there, at the edge of the road running through the Zakaz woods, that his body lies.

2

Youth

Brought up by tutors and governesses at home, Leo Tolstoy was educated like all children in the Russian aristocracy. French became his second language; he learned English and German proficiently, as well. His studies included music, mathematics, history, literature, and the natural sciences. There were lessons in horseback riding and fencing. In his youth the foundation was laid for a superbly strong and athletic body, and his passion for physical exercise never left him.

But his face was not attractive. His nose was broad, his lips were thick, and his gray eyes were small. His hair was unruly, and, as a child, he was stout. Shyness concerning his "ugliness" coupled with his sophisticated upbringing resulted in a curious kind of self-confidence.

There is an incident in the autobiographical *Childhood* in which the mother says: "Remember, Nikolenka, that no one will love you for your face, so you must try to be a clever and good boy." Tolstoy has his hero comment: "Those words not only convinced me that I was no beauty but also that I should certainly be a good and clever boy." That is precisely what he became — sometimes too clever, or at least too self-confident. Once, when he was fascinated by the idea of flying, he jumped out of an upstairs window, falling eighteen feet to the courtyard below. He was unconscious for nearly a day but showed no ill effects afterward.

From the time he was nine, life began to change. Death took away his father, suddenly; he collapsed in the street in Tula in the summer of 1837. Grandmother Tolstoy died the following year. Aunt Alexandra died in 1841. In the meantime, the family began to spend winters in Moscow and only summers at Yasnaya Polyana. Family losses coupled with the variety of his new experiences contributed to his reflectiveness and the development of his meditative nature. Consciousness of death is a theme that dominates many of Tolstoy's later works, but it was present in his thoughts from the beginning. His mother had been taken from him when he was two; while he could barely remember the event, the significance of it was combined with the experience of other deaths in the moving scenes with which *Childhood* is concluded.

His father's sister Aunt Pelageya became the guardian

of the Tolstoy children. She chose to remove them — with cartloads of equipment, supplies, and servants — from their country house to her own home in Kazan. This was in 1841, just after Leo's thirteenth birthday. He continued to live there for five and a half years. Kazan held the seat of much of Russia's venerated history, but it had gone into decline. However, Leo was the grandson of a former governor of the province, and his aunt's home was a social center for "the best people." While Leo lived there, his aunt's main concern was for his position in society. She saw to it that all three of Leo's older brothers attended Kazan University, while he was prepared under special teachers, for the university's entrance examinations. Leo was to be educated for the diplomatic corps. He had no particular conviction for that career, but, under his aunt's pressure, the teen-aged boy had to choose some profession that seemed appropriate to his family's position.

He failed the entrance examination on his first try, in the spring of 1844. Although he had passed the tests in modern languages brilliantly, he did poorly in history, geography, mathematics, Latin, and religion. There is something striking to note about the unsatisfactory showing he made on the religion examination. In later years Tolstoy remembered that, on the day when he was to take the test, he suddenly had the feeling that everything he had ever been taught about religion was a lie.

But the lure of the gay life of a university student was

enough to spur him on. He crammed for the exams again all that summer, and in the fall, shortly after he turned sixteen, he was admitted as a qualified student. University life meant anything but hard studying to him. He took it mainly to play the role of "the dandy." He started smoking and sported the most fashionable clothes. He rode around town on a smart new horse and spent more of his time in the gymnasium or at theaters, balls, concerts, and dinner-parties than at studying. At the end of the year, it was no surprise he was refused admission to the next level of university work. This distressed him more than he admitted, but, rather than face it squarely, he transferred from the course of studies for the diplomatic corps to the Law School.

During the following two years, when Nikolai graduated and entered the army, Leo moved out of his aunt's home and established separate bachelor quarters with his other two brothers and their servants. While the university proved to be less and less satisfying to him, it was during these remaining years in Kazan that he can be said to have begun educating himself. For all his extracurricular activities, he spent a great deal of time reading — not only the novels of Dumas, Dickens, Sterne, and Gogol, among many others, but also the more demanding books of such philosophers as Voltaire, Rousseau, and Hegel; works of political science; and the *New Testament.* By the time he was sixteen he no longer believed the religious instruction of his childhood, but he was soon to begin keeping his diary, and one can readily discover in it the stage of his continuing search for the truths that would replace what he had come to understand was false. He believed in the existence of God but not in any of the Church's supposed implications drawn from that existence. He admired the complexity of systematic rational thought demonstrated by philosophers, but he recognized early in his youth that: *"It is easier to write ten volumes of philosophy than to put a single precept into practice."* At the core of that observation is the main concern of Tolstoy's spiritual quest. It is not only grasping truth, understanding things correctly, that matters; it is more important to be able to *act* in harmony with truth, that is, to live up to one's ideals. The goal of life is *self-perfection,* and, therefore, thought and action, belief and practice, must proceed hand in hand, each helping the other to improve. The university student was beginning to lay the groundwork for the program of a lifetime.

He was dissatisfied and unsuccessful as a university student. In 1847, when Sergei and Dmitri were to finish their studies and leave, Leo determined to abandon Kazan without graduating. Perhaps he was as much influenced by his lack of social success as he was by his disappointment with academic life. At the university he could blame his lack of interest on the dullness of the professors and their routine courses. But how could he explain away the fact that in "society" — for all his efforts to be a dashing gay blade — he was treated as a "bear?" He re-

mained shy and awkward throughout his youth and tried
to compensate for his self-consciousness by eccentricities
of behavior which only made the rejection more certain.
The attractive young ladies he tried to pursue found him
boring; he had no conventional small talk. He was a
poor dancer and his clothes never seemed to fit him properly, no matter how elegantly tailored. Certainly as a result of his lack of social success he comforted himself
with all the means of "living it up" that money could
buy: gambling, drinking, and frequenting loose women.
He did everything with such a degree of intensity and
compelling ambition to excel (he performed his calis-
thenics, for example, with the intention of becoming "the
strongest man in the world") that even in debauchery he
longed to outdo others. In the end, he became ill. He
recognized his failure in Kazan's social life. He wanted
to escape.

By this time, the division of his parents' many properties had been completed. Leo inherited Yasnaya Polyana
and several smaller estates. This included more than five
thousand acres of land along with 350 male serfs and
their families. His intention was to return to his country
home and fulfill his responsibilities as a landowner. He
was then nineteen years old.

Part of his plan was to continue his own moral and
intellectual education on a schedule of studies he had
drawn up for himself. Part of his plan was to become a
devoted master of his property and serfs. But his efforts

Tolstoy at the age of twenty.

to aid the peasants — his attempts to improve them through schooling or proposals for how they should live generally — met with the resistance of their disbelief, cunning, and resentment. It is not simply a question of whether he was too young or inexperienced at the time. Rather, as he rightly began to perceive, the question of how influence for improvement might be effective was intimately bound up with why the relationships between masters and serfs were what they were. Not yet ready to pursue the problems radically, he felt as unfulfilled by his first year as master of the estate as he had felt in Kazan, and he was lonelier — without his brothers, fellow students, or society friends.

In October, after his twentieth birthday, he took off for Moscow. The life of pleasure there was much more intensified than it had been in Kazan, and he achieved a little more social poise and self-assurance. At first he wrote to Auntie Tatyana one letter after another in which he assumed the pose of the bored young man about town. But soon enough the blasé manner gave way to his self-incriminations for the wastrel life. Instead of returning to stay in the country, he spent the following year in St. Petersburg. In fact, it was there that his passion for gambling at cards led him almost to the edge of financial ruin. He was quite unable to determine how best to live his life. At one moment he flung himself into study with the intention of entering the University of St. Petersburg; at the next, he thought he should become a cadet in the

Guards; or with equal verve he considered devoting his life to music. The revolutions of 1848 erupted and exploded across the map of Europe, igniting in the hearts of numerous Russians hopes of political reforms and inspiring dreams of rebellion. But all of the revolutionary activity passed Tolstoy by. He had written in his Kazan diary that "I would be the unhappiest of mortals if I could not find a purpose in life...." But his diaries now showed that — for all his elaborate plans and schedules, rules and exhortations — he had yet to find his purpose.

Oblivious of the political, intellectual, and social ferment in the St. Petersburg of 1848, the world he lived in was that of fashionable drawing rooms, exclusive clubs, and aristocratic parties. He fenced, wrestled, rode, and practiced gymnastics. At night he went to shady establishments of entertainment or made love to the gypsy girls in their haunts on the outskirts of the city.

Still, in the same period, the first hints of the creative artist he was to become gradually became apparent. He observed the life about him with the keenness and intelligence of an unusual mind, and his diaries show that he was beginning to appreciate the difference between making a random record and making the selection, arrangement, and interpretation that is indispensible to art. Until this period he had written youthful reflections on philosophic and religious issues, analyses of music, and rules for his behavior. He now began to show a serious interest in the possibilities of literature. He made attempts to write stories of gypsy life, of a dream, of a hunt, of his first experiences as a landowner, and a detailed account of a day in the life of a man about town.

But, on the whole, he considered the years of his youthful philandering and posturing in Moscow and St. Petersburg totally wasted. His efforts to establish himself in "high society" resulted neither in the suitable marriage nor in the government position that he fancied for himself. Ultimately disillusioned with his foolish way of life, he decided to return to Yasnaya Polyana in the spring of 1851, because his brother Nikolai would be home on a visit. He was not yet to remain there for any length of time, but the consequences of his next departure led him closer to finding his "purpose in life."

3

The Crucial Turning Point

Until the age of twenty-two, Count Leo Tolstoy lived the conventional life of a nineteenth-century Russian aristocrat. Pampered by a large, loving, and generous family, protected from the world of ordinary necessities by his wealth, social position, and isolation, he had grown into manhood with a full array of high ideals and great personal expectations — but without any knowledge of how they might be put into practice or any clear idea of how he should find his way in the world. The reunion with his beloved brother Nikolai unexpectedly pointed the way.

They had not seen each other for four years. As an officer in the Imperial Army, Nikolai was stationed in the Caucasus mountains. Together once again at Yasnaya Polyana, Nikolai suggested that Leo accompany him back to his post and visit with him *on the frontier*. Eager for adventure and happy to cleanse himself of his dissipated life, Leo leapt at the idea with the greatest enthusiasm. To the frontier...!

By analogy to life in America at this time, we get an idea of what "the frontier" meant. In 1851 Russia was expanding south and east, just as the United States was expanding south and west. The battle of the frontier consisted of driving back or conquering the native tribes. In the American South the Cherokee, the Seminole, the Shawnee, the Chickasaw, the Osage, and other tribes had been subdued or driven westward. In the Midwest the Sauk and the Foxes, the Kickapoo, the Winnebago, and others had been conquered. But in New Mexico the Navahos still threatened the American settlements. They raided and plundered the new towns, terrified and stole from the forts. The peace treaties, cautiously agreed to with great difficulty, could not do much to change the situation, despite the fact that, farther west, California was already being settled by emigrants from the east coast. For this reason Fort Defiance was established in the Navaho country in 1851. And yet it was not until 1864, when Colonel Kit Carson was sent to round them up, that the Navahos stopped harassing the settlers.

A similar situation existed in the Caucasus. Mountains as glorious as the Rockies, they were located along the frontier of the expanding Russian empire. While the government had taken control of the territory called

Georgia on the other side of the mountains, between the Caspian and the Black seas, in the mountain areas themselves there remained unfriendly native tribes of Mohammedans, who continued to make forays against the Russian outposts.

For Count Leo Tolstoy to join his brother in returning to the frontier was comparable to a young New England aristocrat, accustomed to the comforts of Boston, New York, and Philadelphia, to journey along with a member of the Union troops to a truly remote outpost in New Mexico or elsewhere in the Far West, where warfare with native Indians was frequent, savage, and inconclusive. To a pampered youth this was the first taste of "real life."

Ordinarily speaking, the concept of "real life" is a much overrated and abused idea; but, to members of an exceptionally fortunate social and economic class, it can mean their introduction to circumstances over which they have no control — situations in which the manners they've been brought up with no longer hold sway — and to actions from simpler motives, with more straightforward expressions and with cruder consequences than they'd been accustomed to. For a person who has been protected and catered to in his earliest years, "real life" means a tougher and rougher life in which to test his capacity to accommodate to people and situations new to him, under circumstances that are not arranged for his comfort and pleasure. Such an experience is the chance for a privileged youth to grow up. It is the challenge and the opportunity for a "gilded youth" to become a man.

Accompanying his brother to the Caucasus was just such a chance for Leo Tolstoy. They left home in April 1851, traveling first through Moscow and Kazan and later by boat down the great Volga river to Astrakhan, on the Caspian Sea. It took them a month to make the trip of more than a thousand miles, and at the end of it, when they arrived at the Cossack village in which Nikolai's unit was stationed, Leo found himself in the heart of the wild, mountainous, frontier country. The Caucasus were as renowned in story, fable, and song for the Russian mind as the Rockies and the Wild West were to Americans at the same time. Land of rugged beauty: mountain peaks and cliffs, rushing torrents, unexplored forests, fierce native tribesmen and their splendid-looking, hearty women. It filled young Leo with a sense of freedom from the artificial and sophisticated ways of life that he thought were the only ones appropriate to a man of his position. The lack of civilization, as he had been accustomed to it, meant release from the previous expectations he had set up for himself. It was his chance to discover his best self —his true self.

During the two and a half years he lived there in Russia's "Wild West," Tolstoy hunted deer, wolves, wild boar, hares and pheasants; he made occasional visits to other villages, forts, and towns; he kept a diary and wrote his first stories; he fought with the army; he meditated upon the ways in which to guide his future. He learned a great deal from the way of life of the Cossacks with whom he lived.

At first he was not directly involved with the army. He took lodgings in the village — a line of reed-thatched log cabins along a single street. This home was remarkable enough for a youth accustomed to the forty-two rooms and thirty domestic servants of his Yasnaya Polyana mansion. But more important was the fact that he lodged in the hut of an extraordinary man, unlike anyone Tolstoy had ever known. This was Epishka Sekhin, eighty years old, giant-sized, powerful (with a bushy beard, dyed red) and striking in the ragged hunting clothes of the frontier. Sekhin had been a skilled horse thief and a slayer of the enemy in his youth. He was called "a daring fellow" — the expression of highest praise among his people. In his old age he still showed his great lust for life, for the pleasures of drinking, gambling, making merry with women, singing native songs, and telling tales. He taught Tolstoy hunting and woodcraft, and he told endless yarns that showed his unrestrained, happy, natural philosophy of a life of simple pleasures. Tolstoy characterized him in a masterful short novel, *The Cossacks,* which he began to write at that time but did not finish until some ten years later.

The very word "Cossack," which comes from the Turkish, originally meant "adventurer." That was what the Turks called the Russian tribes living along their frontier and on the limitlessly wide, fertile plains of southern

Russia — for they were swindlers and thieves, exceptionally skilled horsemen, fighters, and great drinkers, proud to the point of tribal arrogance, primitive and haughty. Independent of rule by the Czar until the beginning of the nineteenth century, the Cossacks now continued to fight their traditional enemies, the Mohammedans, alongside the Imperial troops.

Gradually, as young Tolstoy became more familiar with the Cossacks, as well as with his brother's fellow officers, he also took part in their military actions. The first time was a raid against the hill tribes in the summer of 1851. He went along as a volunteer. The enemy slowly retreated before the advancing troops and, as with the suppression of the American Indians, the government forces then sacked the village that had been abandoned. When they withdrew, their return route was menaced by snipers all the way back. Tolstoy recorded in his diary that he had not acted well under fire, that somehow he was more afraid of the Russian Major General who commanded the raid than he was of the enemy. However, the officers with whom he served said he had behaved courageously, and they urged him to apply for a position in the army immediately.

Although Nikolai, too, encouraged him to do so, Leo thought it over for four months before agreeing. There were many distractions and many alternatives. He had numerous reservations to undertaking a military life. Essentially it was this: while military action gathers up all of a man's physical and moral consciousness and concentrates it with unique intensity upon a single purpose, presumably something unselfishly worth achieving — the truth remains that, except for periods of combat, military life consists of a mind-dulling routine and a series of demands through regimented discipline that offend the dignity of an intelligent (let alone a particularly sensitive) human being. Tolstoy wavered. He wrote his Auntie Tatyana that he had not yet decided between committing himself to military or civil service. He gambled; he caroused with the gypsies and the attractive Cossack women; he hunted; he sketched and he read a great deal; and, above all, he continued to write, to meditate on his relation with God and on how to overcome his failings.

In the fall he left for the nearby town of Tiflis to take the army entrance examination. His excessively wild life had made him ill again, and much of the two months he remained in Tiflis were spent under the treatment of a doctor and in convalescence. It was there that he completed the first part of *Childhood.* A few months after his twenty-third birthday, he wrote Auntie Tatyana:

You recall the advice you once gave me: to write novels. Well, I've followed it, and my endeavors, about which I shall speak to you presently, are literary. I don't know whether what I write will ever see the light of day; but it is work that amuses me, and I have persevered too long now to abandon it.

Thus was the imminent appearance of the greatest master of Russian literature first announced.

In January of 1852 Tolstoy passed the examination to qualify as a cadet and become a noncommissioned officer of artillery, assigned to his brother's brigade. Now a soldier in uniform, he participated in the savage fighting in February, miraculously escaping death when a shell struck the wheel of the cannon he was aiming. It was proposed more than once that he receive the Cross of St. George for his bravery, but his gambling, chess-playing, and carousing late into the night got in the way. He once slept through the medal-awarding ceremony and was put in the guardhouse instead.

Throughout this period he worked hard at his writing and continued to record the stages of his self-examinations in his diary. He had a conviction of greatness and sensed that he was destined to use his powers for the betterment of humanity, but he feared this might be merely the mirage that lures many ambitious young men. It is a hopeful desire more than it is a rational idea. Only the most exceptionally compelled youths turn that hope into a reality. And it is only after they have done so that it is said in retrospect that they "always" were certain to become great men. When one has still to prove himself, even he cannot be certain. He can only wish to accomplish greatness — and make himself work harder.

In London during 1850 Charles Dickens published his novel *David Copperfield.* Because Tolstoy knew English, he was able to read it shortly after it was published. It is a wonderfully moving novel of childhood, despite the fact that it is somewhat melodramatic and sentimental. Tolstoy had great sympathy with English literature and considered himself especially indebted to the writings of Lawrence Sterne; however, there is no doubt that *David Copperfield* had a greater influence on his writing *Childhood* than any other book.

Literary influence is almost impossible to measure when truly original creative writing is examined. It is easy to measure when the earlier work inspires an imitation. But, from one man of genius to another, the essential "influence" amounts to appreciation for some particular quality of excellence which encourages a similar attempt to be original. In this case it was the warmheartedness of the author and the nature of the subject matter that influenced Tolstoy, rather than the style or the plot in Dickens' book. The degree to which Dickens had made the story of a child's life fascinating spurred Tolstoy on. Unlike the English novel, *Childhood* is not melodramatic at all, and there is no taint of false sentiment in it. It re-creates a child's inner life more than it presents a view of the world about him. In these respects, *Childhood* is not only different from *David Copperfield,* it is different from any account of childhood that had ever been written before. Simple as it appears to be in language and in the experiences it relates, there is a great wealth of concerns that run through it: the life of the

landed gentry, the love of living close to nature, awareness of the development of erotic feelings, the effort to
be honest even in complex social situations, the relations
between masters and servants, the presence of a half-mad
religious believer, the tension of "growing pains," and
finally the incomprehensible fact of death. All of these
are woven together — on a small scale, but most artfully
— so that they reflect the richness of a full life that contains them all.

Tolstoy worked on the book for more than a year,
either early in the morning or late at night during the
days when he was on duty with his military battery, out
hunting, or continuing his rather uninhibited life of
pleasure. In July 1852 he sent the completed manuscript
to the editor of *Contemporary,* the leading Russian literary magazine of the day. Two months later he received
an enthusiastic reply; the novel was accepted for publication. It appeared at the end of October, and, in spite of
the fact that Tolstoy was distressed and angered by
changes in the title and text made by the editor and the
government censors, the novel received widespread, glow-
ing praise. He did not sign his full name to the book,
merely the initials "L. T." This intrigued all of the major
Russian literary figures, including Turgenev and Dostoevsky, as well as the less important but passionate followers
of literary developments. They wondered who the remarkably talented author was who had secured the attention and appreciation of a large audience of sincerely

interested readers with the appearance of his first published work.

Tolstoy then sent a second piece to *Contemporary,* an account of his military experiences in the Caucasus called *The Raid.* While it had some of the patriotic "poetry" that made the literature of such frontier actions popular, Tolstoy introduced into it elements of criticism which foreshadow his position years later as one of the world's foremost critics of war.

On his twenty-fourth birthday, still uncertain of his future, Tolstoy noted in his diary that he had "done nothing" so far with his life. He struggled with ideas of God and of how to live his life in the service of humanity — still unsure whether this might best be brought about through literary work, contributing to social and political progress, or in some other way. He worked hard on *Boyhood,* as a sequel to *Childhood,* continued writing of his experiences at Yasnaya Polyana — *The Novel of a Russian Landowner* — and finished several stories — including *Christmas Eve, The Woodfelling* — while he stayed on in his minor position in the army. Early in the winter of 1853 he participated in the campaign against the hill tribes again, only this time it was a major attack, and it broke the resistance of the enemy. When he was not involved with such general efforts or with the smaller-scale scouting forays (during one of which he was almost captured), he often wandered aimlessly among the villages and towns of the neighborhood, amusing himself with women and gambling, or hunting with his Cossack friends.

He had been recommended for promotion because of his bravery, but the commission was slow to come through. Russia had declared war on Turkey in the fall of 1853. He wrote to a relative, Prince Gorchakov, who commanded the armies on the Danubian front, asking for a transfer. His brother Nikolai had resigned from the service, and Leo felt lonely for the kind of friend who could understand his intimate concerns; he felt "unloved."

In January 1854 he received news of transfer to an artillery brigade on the Danube, and he was given a furlough before taking up active duty. Happily he set out on the long trip to Yasnaya Polyana. It was midwinter and the blizzard he lived through on the way home was the occasion for his story *The Snow Storm*.

By the end of these two and a half years in the Caucasus, he was still uncertain about the shape his future life would take — despite the fact that he already offered proof of the most important element in his make-up as a writer: he knew how to transmute the raw material of his immediate experiences into works of art, through the persistence of hard work and the magical, transforming powers of his reflective imagination. He had become "a daring fellow" — so praised by his Cossack friends; and he was about to become *a very daring fellow* as far as the rest of the world was concerned. He was already a writer working for the well-being of mankind, without knowing it.

4

Sevastopol

For more than a century Russia had warred with Turkey in every generation. During the period of nation-building she fought to expand her territory southward in hopes of commanding all the land surrounding the Black Sea. This would give her direct access to the Mediterranean. By the end of the last war in 1829, the Turkish government — the Ottoman empire — corrupt and decaying, had forfeited to Russia all of the territory along the northern half of the Black Sea, from Bessarabia on the west, through the peninsula of Crimea, to the Caucasus on the east. In the Balkans, Greece became a kingdom independent of the Ottoman empire in 1829, but the Turks still controlled the remaining territory bordering on the Austrian empire. Now, in 1853, Czar Nicholas I made new demands.　On the trumped-up issue of Russian rights to protect Christians in the Ottoman empire (especially in Jerusalem), Russia invaded the Balkan territories surrounding the city of Bucharest. The Turks, however, were in no hurry to fight, and so it was to a peaceful Bucharest that the newly promoted ensign Count Leo Tolstoy arrived in March of 1854. This was the month in which the "phony" aspect of the war ended, for England and France broke off relations with Russia, and the Crimean War became the first international calamity since Waterloo ended the Napoleonic wars in 1815.

Tolstoy himself did not come to understand the reasons for the war until some years later, but, when he did, he argued forcefully that it had started with the greed of the Czar combined with his desire to channel Russian political energies away from internal reforms. France became involved because Napoleon III felt personally offended by the Czar and because France had vast commercial and political interests in the Ottoman empire. England, soon to take over the Suez Canal, was concerned only with protecting its command of the Mediterranean. Thus, England and France became allies for the first time in centuries, and the degenerate Turkish government was content to let them fight the war in its place. The Austrian empire, unhappy over the possibility of further Russian influence in the Balkans, moved into the territories surrounding Bucharest as the Russians evacuated it under pressure of these combined forces. At this point Nicholas died, and his successor, Alexander II, considered bringing the war to an end; but, by delay and indecision, the needless campaign not only continued but became infinitely worse.

This catastrophe of political bungling reached its climax in the siege of Sevastopol, the principal port city of the Crimea.

Bombardment of the city began in October and continued for a whole year until the city surrendered the following September. This was the beginning of trench warfare, with soldiers of both sides living through the miserable winter in the mud-filled dugouts on either side of the fortifications of Sevastopol. It was also the last of the wars in which many amateur officers — given their positions purely for social reasons — ineptly and inefficiently commanded the common soldiers. During some of the siege Tolstoy was exposed to the worst dangers, constantly under fire.

At first, keenly aware of the necessity to bolster the spirits of the soldiers, he proposed to edit and publish a popular magazine for the education of the troops. Permission was refused by the Czar. Tolstoy's public concerns were still patriotic, and he seemed hardly conscious of the reactionary and oppressive nature of the government. But even then his private notes were filled with criticism of the corrupt "military mind." Through the course of the winter he produced a work of descriptive

Tolstoy as a Crimean Army officer.

journalism of the highest order, *Sevastopol in December,*
still fervid with patriotic ardor but, nevertheless, offering
a clear distinction between an outsider's misleading conception of the glory of war and the reality of the misery
that a participant knows. It shows:

> . . . war not with its orderly, beautiful, and brilliant
> ranks, its music and beating drums, its waving ban-
> ners, its generals on prancing horses, but war in its
> real aspects of blood, suffering, and death. . . .

When it was published in June, the Czar was said to
have been so moved by it that he ordered the author's
life to be well guarded. As a matter of fact, Tolstoy had
been assigned to a battery of mountain guns in a somewhat safer location by then (but through no intervention
of the Czar's). During this time he read a great deal of
European literature — Goethe, Heine, Balzac, and Thackeray, for example — and wrote in his diary a remarkably
prophetic passage:

> Yesterday a conversation about divinity and faith
> suggested to me a great, a stupendous idea to the
> realization of which I feel capable of dedicating my
> whole life. This is the idea — the founding of a new
> religion corresponding to the development of man-
> kind: the religion of Christ, but purged of all
> dogma and mysteriousness, a practical religion, not
> promising future bliss but realizing bliss on earth.
> I understand that to bring this idea to fulfillment
> the conscientious labor of generations toward this

end will be necessary. One generation will bequeath the idea to the next, and some day fanaticism or reason will achieve it. *Consciously* to contribute to the union of man and religion is the basic idea which I hope will improve me.

It is important to remember this insight of his during the time of the Crimean War, for it indicates that Tolstoy's concern for "a new religion" was already present at this stage of his life.

The writing of his *Sevastopol in May* reflects a dramatic change in his outlook. This is no continuation of his patriotic naïveté, no paean of praise to the modest, courageous, self-sacrifice of the common soldier. By July, when he had completed it, he was quite ready to recognize it for what it is: a searing indictment of war. It is a story that describes war from the inside. By implication, the question it raises is perfectly clear: How can people who proclaim themselves to be Christian murder each other?

The government censors objected to the story so strongly that it was allowed to be published only after they had revised it, and therefore Tolstoy withdrew his name as author. He now conceived of war as not only stupid and criminal but as the ultimate antithesis to every Christian belief. When his final story of the muddling senselessness and savagery of the war, *Sevastopol in August,* was published in 1855, the censor permitted only four of its twenty-seven sections to appear.

By September the military situation had become hopeless. With Sevastopol in ruins, the remnants of the army were withdrawn, and the Czar sued for peace. The political and diplomatic consequences of the carnage of the Crimean War amount simply to this: the Balkan area surrounding Bucharest became the independent kingdom of Rumania, and Russian warships were prohibited from sailing the Black Sea — a restriction that was lifted three years later.

Tolstoy resigned from the army in November, shortly after arriving in St. Petersburg. He had not only become a pacifist, he had become something of a literary hero. The unusual literary mastery, evident from his first published writings, were now joined with the moral seriousness that had previously appeared only in the reflective passages of his diaries. He was welcomed with open arms by the members of the "literary world" of the capital.

5

Europe

Tolstoy took them by storm and ended by stormily turning his back on them. He behaved as the absolute individualist among antlike group members. Through Turgenev and the editor of *Contemporary,* he met all of the leading novelists, playwrights, essayists, and poets, but he considered that the purposes which divided them — into liberals, on the one hand, and radicals, on the other — were equally self-deluding and equally doomed. He found the whole literary establishment "disgusting" and wrote in his diary: ". . . I want affection, friendship, but they are not capable of it." Within a month, he came to be thought of as a "savage." And still he did establish certain friendships which lasted the rest of his life, especially with men, but also with a remarkable woman, his distant cousin Countess Alexandra Tolstoy, who was part of the literary and social world at the Czar's court.

His short novel *Two Hussars* was published at the beginning of 1856, followed in the spring by two short stories. In September his collected *Army Tales* were brought out in book form, followed shortly by *Youth,* which completed the work begun by *Childhood* and *Boyhood.*

In March the young Czar announced that the government had under consideration plans for freeing the serfs (although the emancipation was actually still five years off), and he suggested that in the meanwhile individual landowners might take independent action. Tolstoy brusquely abandoned the capital with the intention of putting into practice some of the theories the serf-owning members of the literary world only talked about, and, on the day of his arrival at Yasnaya Polyana, he called a meeting of all his male serfs.

He explained that the estate was mortgaged and that until he was out of debt he could not free them; but he offered them each twelve acres of land — half as an outright gift, half mortgaged to him for thirty years, at the end of which time they would own their own land free and clear. The serfs rejected the offer, however, believing that when the Czar freed all the serfs he would simply *give* them the land. Tolsoty's problem was how to balance his moral conviction that the serfs should be freed and given an opportunity to support themselves, against his common-sense wish not to ruin himself economically.

Somewhat bitter and perplexed by the failure of his plan, Tolstoy remained in the country during the summer. His brother Dmitri had died. He visited his now married sister, he read and wrote steadily, practiced his gymnastics, hunted, and pursued many of the local women. He was twenty-eight and still unmarried. His recent romantic interests in the capital had been no more successful than his earlier attractions in Kazan or Moscow. During the next few months he "courted" the daughter of a neighboring landowner, but all too deliberately. He could not believe she offered sufficient promise of the personal and family happiness he longed for. He retreated to Moscow and then to St. Petersburg again. In November he left for France.

The "Grand Tour" of Western Europe had been thought of for two centuries as the final polishing stage to an aristocratic youth's formal — and informal — education. In 1857 Tolstoy was no callow youngster, but somehow between his first and second trips to Europe his long youth drew to an end. In Paris he attended lectures at the Sorbonne, visited museums and major tourist attractions, but also he found all doors open to him and he took his pleasures at every level. While he worked at his writings as persistently as ever and read a great number of books, he also traveled in Switzerland with his serious "Granny" (as he jokingly called the Countess Alexandra), and later in Germany and the low countries. He hiked in the Alps, danced and sang, attended theaters and concerts, gambled and flirted. There was a period of one week during which he made a trip with Turgenev and they worked at their own writings while sharing a room in Dijon. But it ended with a fight, as usual. Despite their respect for each other, and their wish to get along, they were temperamentally incompatible, and diametrically opposed on too many issues of importance.

Turgenev believed in art for its own sake; Tolstoy conceived of it as a means to other ends. This difference between them was particularly ironic at that time — when Turgenev's liberal position had established him as a leading writer of social significance, whereas Tolstoy's works (with the exception of the Sevastopol pieces) were criticized for lack of social or political purpose. Still, it was just such a public issue that turned Tolstoy away from Paris. He witnessed the execution of a criminal; the sight of the guillotining was so repellent and the idea of capital punishment so appalling to him that he left the city. Turgenev makes the point, in his own famous account of an "invitation to a beheading," of his decision, at the last moment, *not to view it.* Perhaps, symbolically, here is the marked contrast between the realist and the romantic. It certainly shows the difference between the moralist and the aesthete.

Returning to Russia in midsummer, Tolstoy went directly to the estate — of which he had now been master for ten years. He was full of new plans: the value of his property would go up with the addition of orchards and new buildings; there would be a regular policy of allowing serfs to buy their freedom; he would establish a school for the children of the village. Yet, despite his enthusiasm, the next few months proved a strain. He played Beethoven, read Homer, and continued to write; he visited friends and relatives; but he was generally either bored or sad. He understood why: he was still without a wife and family.

During the fall and winter he stayed in Moscow. Often he visited with the family of the court physician, Dr. Bers, whose wife was a life-long friend of his. They had charming and attractive daughters, and Tolstoy noted in his diary: "If Sonya were sixteen and not fourteen, I would propose to her at once." He was then thirty years old. It is impossible to know whether Tolstoy had any premonition when he wrote that remark in his diary that Sonya Bers was to become the woman of his life. In any event, he spent the season as usual: between working out at the gym and being entertained in the best homes. One achievement of the stay incidentally, was his joining with other music lovers to organize a society which later developed into the renowned Moscow Conservatory.

In the spring he was back home again. He immersed himself in peasant life, even learning to plow the fields himself. He exchanged visits with Turgenev, was visited by "Granny," and relaxed in the company of the aging Auntie Tatyana. He had an affair with a serf, Aksinya, who later bore him a son; but this only made him wish more for a woman of his own station whom he could lovingly marry. In his writing, he was beginning to come to grips with the problems of how to merge his moral concerns with the creation of works of art. His most recent stories, *Three Deaths* and *Family Happiness,* were not well received by the public, but the use of literature to express truth as he saw it was clearly his attitude toward writing, regardless of what the "literary world" thought of his efforts.

In a country of sixty million "souls" in which only one per cent of the population is literate, what is the purpose of literature? he asked himself. It would be more significant to stop writing fiction — mere amusements for the idle — and teach the young how to read and how to think for themselves. With the exception of a few haphazard courses of instruction given by priests, peasant children had no opportunity for any schooling. There was no free or compulsory education in Russia. The more he considered the idea, the more determined he became to establish a school. It would be free to all the neighboring children who wanted to come. Tolstoy had a perfectly natural, easy manner with children, and they loved him readily. He took to teaching them as happily as a bear takes to honey.

When Tolstoy was successful at planting trees on his own estate, he proposed to the government a national program for reforestation. Similarly, within six months of starting his first school (for fifty children), he had already turned his thoughts to improving education throughout the country. He considered publishing a journal devoted to the problems of educational theory and practice; but, sharply aware that Russia respected ideas about these problems only when they came from other European sources, he decided to study foreign teaching methods. In July 1860 he left for Europe again to undertake the survey — and to visit his brother Nikolai, who was trying to recover from tuberculosis.

During the first months in Germany, he saw how children were taught by rote and by threat. He loathed the fact that they were beaten and debased (and made to spend time saying prayers for the King). He was beginning to believe that in education as in other human relations: "the chief things are equality and freedom." But his research was sadly interrupted; Nikolai's health deteriorated even further, and on doctors' advice Leo took him to the south of France. It was there, in September, that Nikolai died.

No one's death seems to have affected Tolstoy as profoundly as Nikolai's. His mother and father had died; Dmitri was gone; comrades in the army had been killed by his side. But, of all these, it was Nikolai whom he had known best and loved the most, a young man in the prime of life, a potentially highly talented writer himself, with all the worldly advantages that fortune, breeding, and self-respect might bestow on a favored son: dead at the age of thirty-seven. Surely the "meaning of life" is bound up or fused with an understanding of death. Tolstoy had tried to understand. In *Childhood* death remained incomprehensible; only the grief of the survivors and the horror of not understanding are expressed there. *Army Tales* is filled with self-sacrificing courage and appreciation of pain; but the question of meaning is clouded by criticism of the unnecessary political and military conditions resulting in death. In the short story *Three Deaths*, written in 1858, Tolstoy had tried to probe further. He presented the last days in the lives of a wealthy woman, a laborer, and a tree. Both the tree and the common man are intimately involved in nature and willingly let go of their lives, whereas the "educated" and privileged lady, for all her pretense of having been brought to peace by the sacraments of the Church, is in fact unresigned, self-pitying, bitter, and frustrated. The deaths of the tree and the plain old worker yield something to the well-being of the on-going "societies" in which they lived; but the death of the lady makes the members of her "society" seem to shrink or shrivel further into their own egocentric concerns. The story is not completely successful. It is ironic and ambivalent in tone, and inconclusive, since it reflects Tolstoy's thinking only as far as it had come by then. By itself, even Nikolai's death failed to bring Leo to a fuller understanding; indeed, he was only thrown into greater doubt about how well anyone understood the meaning of existence. As he roused himself from his grief, all he could do was to plunge himself more deeply into his own way of life.

Throughout the remainder of the fall he stayed in the south of France. In the winter he made a short tour of Italy. By mid-February he had returned to his purpose of studying education. For two months he visited schools in England, even attending a lecture on education delivered by Dickens himself. He collected textbooks and questioned pupils wherever he went. After England it was Belgium and then Germany again. In Berlin he met a writer named Berthold Auerbach, whose novel *A New Life* had a considerable effect on Tolstoy. He had read it just the year before. It tells the rather romantic story of a count who becomes a village schoolteacher, and who puts into practice a theory of education designed to enable people to become self-regulating, establishing laws for themselves rather than having to go through life being kept within bounds by governmental or religious threats of punishment. In the schoolroom the pupils were allowed complete freedom; everything was done to cultivate each child's sense of his own value — his self-respect and his self-confidence.

Both the moral purpose of this vision of education and its practical methods suited Tolstoy's temperament perfectly. It was an original conception of *progressive education* — written almost exactly a hundred years after Rousseau's *Émile* of 1762. Rousseau's revolutionary novel, proposing that the best way to educate would be by persuasion and guidance rather than by fear, threat, and punishment, was also well known to Tolstoy. His interpretation of these theories, on the basis of which he conducted the school at Yasnaya Polyana, came forty years before the somewhat similar theories of John Dewey, the great American proponent of progressive education.

In April 1861 Tolstoy returned to Russia, having left his last experience of Western Europe behind him. He did not travel abroad again for the rest of his life — that is, for the following fifty years.

6

Fulfillment

Perhaps if Tolstoy had continued to devote himself to the problems of education, he might very well have contributed to making the purposes of schooling more understandable and the methods of teaching more reasonable. It might have been sufficient for a major career. But that was not to be, for a variety of reasons. The school he founded for peasant children at Yasnaya Polyana, which he conducted with the co-operation of like-minded teachers, lasted for only a few years. However, as the direct experience of war led Tolstoy to face the questions of what rights any man has over the life and death of another man, so the direct experience of teaching brought him to confront the problems of what rights any individual has over the inner formation of another. These are

Tolstoy at about age forty.

the disguised assumptions at the heart of any theory of education. Tolstoy's criticism of conventional education is as devastating as his judgment on other aspects of social and political life.

The essence of Tolstoy's objection to all previous approaches to education is that the short-range methods of schooling contradict the long-range purposes of education. At least the *supposed* purposes of teaching are to make a person able to act independently, responsibly (with self-reliance), spontaneously (with originality), and with the passion for a continuing pursuit of knowledge. But the techniques of fear, the demands for obedience, the systems of punishment and rewards, the structure of competition, and the necessity to accumulate stockpiles of irrelevant information — the dead weight of "book-larnin'" — frustrate all of the long-range intentions. Instead, pupils respond in exactly the opposite way: they develop a loathing for learning at the same time that they become passive, herdlike, resentfully un-co-operative, and resistant to any form of social relations but that of "getting their own" in spite of the system.

Teaching so-called scientific knowledge is devalued by the truth that such knowledge is constantly in flux; the "knowledge" of one generation is the errors of the next. Teaching virtuous forms of social and political life is perfectly arbitrary, as the styles vary with the practices of each society, economic class, and nation. The only just education, therefore, is the free cultivation of each individual's own nature, so that he may truly become free to pursue what is not irrelevant but of genuine interest to *him,* and live with others in mutual respect for their characters and their interests, too. Everything depends on respecting the essential goodness of each human being. Without that, all forms of education are self-defeating and produce only the spite-filled robots who occupy the seats in regimented schoolrooms, under duress and only until they are able to escape.

At Yasnaya Polyana the words "Enter and Leave Freely" were printed on a sign over the door of the school. Tolstoy's position — namely, that everything about the children's education was to be done by them *freely* or not at all — rested on the truth that a person either educates himself or forever remains uneducated. A teacher is a person whose only value is to help the student cultivate his native abilities, his natural powers, his own character: pouring a quantity of "knowledge" into a resisting pupil can never have any good result at all.

What Tolstoy has to say here, in his practice at the school and in his dozen essays on education which remain from this period, summarizes the stage to which his thinking had come about human relations in general and anticipates the even more radical positions he would take later. The key to education is *the moral development of a human being;* it is his character that matters, not the "trimmings." By the same token, ultimately, this will become for Tolstoy the key to all human life.

Between 1858 and 1862, Tolstoy appeared to have abandoned literature. He was no longer mentioned in the publications of the literary world as a highly talented and productive writer. He seemed to be in a state of stagnation. Turgenev took it upon himself to lure Tolstoy back to fiction. But that presumption on his part, complicated in numerous ways, led to a break between them that lasted for seventeen years. However, by the fall of 1862, Tolstoy was again at work on short novels. A gambling debt in the beginning of that year led him to promise the completion of *The Cossacks* to a publisher; and he delivered it within a year. The study of peasant life, *Polikushka,* also was finished that fall.

What the critics were incapable, then, of assessing was the way in which Tolstoy's withdrawal from their world enabled him to nourish his own soul. Working with the peasants on his land as well as with the children in the school showed him where satisfaction might best be found for himself — by living in accord with his own nature. His more clearly formulated ideas about God, religion, and social and political life were yet to come forth, but they were being properly fed by his present experiences — remote from the sophisticated concerns of the literati and city elite. And there remained a feature of primary value, of overriding importance, in his character formation which had not yet been supplied. He was still unmarried; the vision of family happiness that he longed to realize, in his own way, on his own terms, remained apparently beyond his grasp.

Until 1862. He was then thirty-four years old. Sonya Bers was eighteen.

During the summer he resumed his visits to the Bers family at their apartments in the Kremlin. Bers's wife had known Tolstoy since childhood (she was only two years older than he), and both were as fond of him as they were admiring and respectful of his fiction. In fact, it was their hope that Tolstoy would marry their eldest daughter, Liza. But, while she was as beautiful and civilized an example of her class as could be imagined, her cool temperament and "intellectual" concerns attracted Tolstoy no more than any of the many appropriate "prospects" he had considered before. It was Sonya who fascinated him.

Sonya combined the impish gaiety and vivacity of her younger sister with the seriousness of the older Liza. Her dark hair framed a face rosy with health, and her large brown eyes expressed her warm-heartedness. She loved literature, music, painting, and children. She adored Count Leo Tolstoy — the author she had read since childhood — passages from whose work she had memorized years before.

Tolstoy fell passionately in love with her but suffered torturously for weeks before he asked her to marry him. He feared that he was too old, too unattractive, that the life he would offer her at Yasnaya Polyana could not be

satisfactory to a "hothouse flower" at the inner circle of
Moscow's highest society. Most of all he feared the blow
it would cause him — not only to his pride, but to his
dreams about family happiness — if she refused him. In
the end, though the Bers family had at first considered his
proposal scandalous, they consented, and all his fantasies
about the promise of happiness with Sonya came true.
She was simply as much in love with him as he was with
her. Each was marrying "the ideal partner." Surely, Tolstoy believed he was taking as a wife a young woman
who would always sympathize with him — that is, feel
as he felt about all things — as fully as she did now.
Surely, Sonya Bers believed she was becoming the wife
of one of the most promising writers of fiction in Russia,
a nobleman, wealthy enough to secure the future for herself and their children in the manner to which she was
accustomed, a distinguished member of the society she
admired without critical reservation. In the beginning
they were both right. Neither of them could have antici-
pated the way in which Tolstoy's mind would develop
after the middle of his life and the response that those
changes would draw from his wife.

They were married within a matter of weeks: on September 23, 1862, and on their wedding night they left
Moscow for Yasnaya Polyana. Within a week, in a letter
to "Granny," he was writing: "I have lived to the age of
thirty-four and did not realize that one may love so and

be so happy." Sonya wrote to her younger sister: ". . . may God give you such happiness as I now enjoy. More does not exist."

But the difficulties of practical adjustments arose quickly enough. She was a city girl, and country ways were crude by her standards. For all the pleasure she took in becoming a countess, none of her friends was about to enjoy it with her; she saw only peasants and rustic neighbors, the people involved in the school, which continued for a little while longer, and the odd creatures who, as interesting passers-by, would call on the master of the estate. The Count himself, after all, had been a self-sufficient bachelor for a long time. He was accustomed to regulating his schedule by his independent interests, whether they were concerned with the farm, his studies, his writing, playing music, or engaging visitors in conversation. In many ways, obviously, he hardly knew what to expect of a wife, and she unquestionably had little idea of what the mistress of such a house in the country and the wife of such a man should expect of herself.

Every husband and wife must face the surprises of living together — which can never be known in advance, no matter how well they believe they are acquainted with each other before marriage. But the Tolstoys' intimate relationship was uniquely complicated by a consequence of one of their most noble characteristics. They were sworn to perfect honesty with each other. They both kept diaries and made them available for each other to read. In anticipation of this future practice, Tolstoy had offered all of his previous diaries to Sonya. This meant that she learned of all his earlier, numerous, and often intense affairs with other women. Of greatest significance among these was the record of his relationship with the peasant woman Aksinya — who was there on the estate, literally under the nose of the young wife from the moment she arrived. Sonya's jealousy was an exaggerated fear on her part, for Tolstoy remained faithful to her throughout their marriage. But it was the understandable response of a young girl to her doubts about the life of an "inveterate" bachelor who was also a man of enormous energy and immense range of interests.

Despite difficulties, they made concessions to each other and began to establish the habits that put their marriage on a firm foundation. They read or played music together in the evenings; she undertook to make clean copies of her husband's manuscripts; he taught her English; they spent the Christmas season in Moscow with her family. But the fear that her love for him was not sufficient, and that therefore she would always stand in danger of losing his love, also became a part of the established pattern.

On June 28, 1863, their first child was born — a son, whom they named Sergei. It was the beginning of "family" in the classic sense Tolstoy had always dreamed of. He bought a herd of sheep, installed a distillery, planted fruit trees, and began to cultivate bees. To improve his property was a goal that Sonya well understood and appreciated; but the improvement of his mind and the cultivation of his spiritual life was an activity of his inward existence that she did not grasp. The resentment she felt toward it in their earliest years, merely because of the time it took him away from her, could only become more intense as its fruits later came to be harvested. But for Tolstoy himself, at the age of thirty-five, in command of all the conditions necessary for the blossoming of his genius, all was ready at last for the appearance of the most important works of his literary life.

7

The World's Greatest Novelist

During the next decade Tolstoy wrote the best novel that has ever been written, *War and Peace,* and then he wrote the second-best novel ever written, *Anna Karenina.*

Of course a judgment of this sort is wide open to dispute; but it makes a reasonable resolution for one side of a literary debate. "Best" here implies both enjoyment and significance, intensity and ramification, the masterful marshaling of fact by a superlative power of interpretation. Because of the credibility of the characters, the compassion of the author's attitudes toward them, and the extraordinary inclusiveness of the scope of these books, they create the ultimate realistic impression which many great critics have tried to express — such as Thomas Mann, who said: *"rarely ever has art so completely given the effect of nature."* These novels do not seem to be works of art; they give the appearance of being life itself.

Perhaps the simplest reason for this is that the primary characteristic of the realist's art is to make explicit what is implicit but inarticulate in all men. There is a passage in *Anna Karenina* that might stand as a touchstone for this artistic approach. The painter Mikhailov is commissioned by Count Vronsky to paint Anna's portrait.

> From the fifth sitting the portrait impressed everyone, especially Vronsky, not only by its likeness, but by its characteristic beauty. It is strange how Mikhailov could have discovered her special beauty. "One needs to know and love her as I have loved her to discover the very sweetest expression of her soul," Vronsky thought, though it was only from this portrait that he had himself learned this sweetest expression of her soul. But the expression was so true that he, and others too, thought they had long known it.

Thus, *beauty* in a work of art derives from being true to nature, and *truth* is what all men can recognize — once it is pointed out to them. But it takes a great artist to point it out.

To say that *War and Peace* is a historical novel would be as inadequate as saying that Homer's *Iliad* is a war story. But Tolstoy developed it out of various ideas for a historical novel. At first the epoch he thought of writing about was somewhat closer to his own. Gradually, however, between 1861 and 1863, as his drafts for the book clearly show, his concern for the conditions that created the character of life in Russia at the middle of the century led him to concentrate on an earlier period in Russian history — survival of the Napoleonic invasion, the years between 1805 and 1814.

His father had fought in the war. Tolstoy called on his family records, memoirs of others, government accounts, eye-witness reports, historical documents of all sorts. The Bers family in Moscow, caught up with his enthusiasm for research, supplied him with many primary source references. He personally consulted well-known historians in Moscow. As early as 1861 he had written to Herzen about his intentions. For a time the book he contemplated was tentatively called *All's Well That Ends Well,* a family novel in the manner of Dickens or Thackeray with merely a "backdrop" of the Napoleonic war. It should be noted that, during Tolstoy's second visit to Western Europe, Herzen had made it possible for him to meet in Brussels the French writer Proudhon, whose book of political science, which much impressed Tolstoy at the time, was entitled *War and Peace.*

In October of 1864 Sonya gave birth to their second child, a daughter. Shortly before, Tolstoy had broken his arm in a riding accident, and at the end of November he went alone to Moscow for an operation to re-set it. While there, the Bers family arranged for an evening at which he read aloud to friends of the family a portion of the novel in manuscript. The tremendously successful impression that it made convinced Sonya (when she read about it in his letter to her) that he should not allow all of the book to be serialized in a magazine nor even commit it to a publisher but rather should publish it himself. Deciding to do this was a business judgment of the greatest importance to the financial future of the family, for the novel earned a sizable fortune.

When it was finally completed — after six years — and appeared, in March 1869, both the critics and the public received it with the enthusiasm called forth only by a sensationally important event. It is the epic of modern civilization in the sense that Homer's *Iliad* is the epic of classical civilization and Dante's *Divine Comedy* is of of the Christian Middle Ages. Woven of many strands representing the peasantry, the aristocracy, the military, and leaders of government, it presents a tapestry of great richness which shows above all else that — regardless of the conflicts between nations, between religious and political ideas, between private hopes and public movements — the essence of life is personal and familial, not public and political. Diplomacy and politics make disasterous demands on individuals during a war, but it is only the suffering, longing, living individual person who matters — not the hollow abstractions called "nations," let alone the ideas of those unfortunately misguided people who are known to us as "great men." *War and Peace* is not only the story of scores of lives but also, over and above the story, a proposal of a unique philosophy of history, one of Tolstoy's most remarkable contributions to thought as well as to literature.

"Reality" resides in the personal experiences of individuals. The frame for all the public action, the condition of the "outside" world which confronts all of the characters, is the struggle between France and Russia; but the pulse of life flows through the veins of the people confronted by this common challenge, and each of them is living out a private design for his or her own meaningfulness quite independent of the public problem. The great battles are there, the advance of Napoleon's troops, the occupation and the burning of Moscow, the retreat, the slaughter and the suffering, all clearly imprinted in the mind of the reader as deep and vivid as a soldier's boot print in the Russian snow. But even more real than that is the life of each individual. Natasha Rostov flowers before our eyes — from the young woman attending her first ball, whom we watch over the course of the years fall in and out of love, then marry and become the mother of a family: hopeful, lively, charming, warmhearted, and gay. Pierre Bezukhov, self-conscious and insecure, probing his way in the world beset with traps for him, matures gradually, through all the stages of thought and action that show how a sensitive human being responds to the demands made upon him by the society he lives in and the needs of his time. Prince Andrei's courage and intelligence, Princess Mary's goodness, General Kutuzov's cunning, Platon Karataev's holiness — these are the human attributes that remain most memorable in the work of art that appears to be "life itself."

And still it is, for all that, a historical novel. Why did Tolstoy find Napoleon's invasion of Russia so significant? Napoleon represented himself as heir to the French Revolution, and that political upheaval is the fountainhead of all the great revolutionary ideas of the nineteenth century. After the establishment of Christianity as the dominant European religion and the development of nations out of the feudalism of the Middle Ages, the idea that *things could be other than they are* had been merely an underground grievance until the explosion of the French Revolution. That event suddenly made manifest to all that the power to "create a new world" was in their hands.

On the intellectual side, the equivalent of the French Revolution was to be found in the writings of the German philosopher Hegel (1770-1831). He argued that "truth" is no more eternal in philosophy or science than established social and political orders are "necessary." He maintained that values are created as the result of conflicts in history. To examine how historical changes bring about new values, patterns, and "orders" in political life as well as in art, social life, law, etc., became the primary concern of the intellectually minded. History was thus made the indispensable key to understanding life, and so the philosophy of history became the dominant abstract enterprise of nineteenth-century intellectual life.

In political economy it led to the writings of Karl Marx; the first volume of his *Capital* was published in 1867. In the natural sciences the most important single innovation incorporating the idea of historical change was Darwin's *Origin of Species,* which appeared in 1859. *War and Peace,* completed in 1869, was written in an atmosphere charged with the attempt to understand the meaning of history. What constitutes the "movements" of historical change? How do they come about? Are they directed toward a purposeful goal? What is in the power of leaders freely to determine, and what is conditioned by forces that are outside anyone's power?

Tolstoy took the position that the great events of historical change do not depend on individual leaders. On the contrary, the so-called Great Men who imagine they are in command of situations are really pawns of powers entirely out of their control. Neither Napoleon nor Czar Alexander I "decided" the shape or the end of the invasion of Russia. Great historical events are so complex in their character that no one reason can be singled out to explain them. As for the purposes of rulers, Tolstoy became convinced, they not only do not work for the good of the people, they actually contribute to their harm. What Tolstoy came to see as the conflicting purposes that flow in opposing directions are: individual people trying to live good lives for themselves, on the one hand, and the drive for power — imaginary as it might be, and destructive as it certainly is — of national "leaders," on the other hand. The laws that govern private lives come to be seen as the sound, eternal conditions of human nature; whereas national-governmental policies, whether they pretend to be serving "progress," the defense of Christianity, nationalism, or whatnot, are both self-deceiving and catastrophic. In a word, philosophy of history is a *fraud*. The only thing that makes life meaningful is the island of individual-family private life that each man secures for himself in a poisonous swamp of public life.

Such ideas contribute to the over-all character of *War and Peace,* but the novel is not only about these ideas, it is about people. What real people seek is their private happiness in the face of the absurdities of political history. The novel presents the life-struggle of a nation through the experiences of families and of individuals, dramatically represented in the most minute detail of their thoughts and feelings as well as in their actions. Preparing to write the book, Tolstoy noted in his diary:

> I read with delight the history of Napoleon and Alexander. At once I was enveloped in a cloud of joy; and the consciousness of the possibility of doing a great thing took hold of my thoughts — to write a psychological novel of Alexander and Napoleon, and of all the baseness, empty words, folly, all the contradictions of these men and of the people surrounding them.

While Tolstoy did in fact achieve this purpose, it is not

the Emperor and the Czar whom the reader remembers best. Rather it is the families of the Bezukhovs, the Rostovs, the Bolkonskis, the Kuragins, the Drubetskoys.

To paraphrase a great epigram of Tolstoy's: "National leaders are all alike; every private person is individual in his own way." It is the love of life of each individual in the novel which makes *War and Peace* such an extraordinary experience — given the scope of the field where they are put to play and the depth of the ideas with which Tolstoy relates them to the world they live in. It still remains very much an open question whether a philosophy of history is possible and how the relations between private life and public life might best be understood, but the implications of the ideas in *War and Peace* have in no sense been refuted by the contributions to thought about these issues during the past century.

For Tolstoy there was an interlude of four years between completing *War and Peace* and commencing to write *Anna Karenina,* during which time he attempted two plays, a comedy called *A Contaminated Family* and *The Nihilist.* Two more sons were born, Ilya in 1866 and Leo in 1869. He read a great deal of philosophy, Schopenhauer for example, and works by numerous religious thinkers. In 1870 he began research for a novel based on the life of Czar Peter the Great, only to abandon it in disgust at the character of the man. Alone on a short trip, he awoke in the middle of the night in the cold horror of recognizing the inevitability of his own death. Every rational person knows that his death is to be expected. But to be aware of it in a logical way is simply "unreal" by contrast with the intensity of the emotional experience by which one believes it. The difference is as great as the difference between *imagining* that part of your body might be amputated and *actually* waking after an operation to discover that your leg, for example, is gone. Belief in the truth of his own death is what Tolstoy experienced. That night of discovery came to be expressed later in his story about the experience called *Diary of a Madman.*

Concentrating on the meaning that future death has for one's life, Tolstoy felt the necessity to come to grips with Christianity, and so he undertook to learn Greek — which he mastered in an impressively short time — in order to study the *New Testament* in the original. In 1871 his fifth child, Marya, was born. By then Sonya's objections to the number of children she had to bear and care for led to a certain emotional distance between them, and in that year Tolstoy's own ill health brought about a physical separation. He traveled south to the Bashkir tribes on the steppes near Samara, took a health cure, and ended by buying a large estate of virgin land in the territory. Once again he became involved with problems of education, and he prepared for publication a primer for use in schools and at home, his *A B C Book*, which continued to be of importance for more than half a century. He became one of the founders of the Society of the

Lovers of Russian Folksongs, at the very time that the irritations of living in Russia had so infuriated him he contemplated the possibility of selling everything he owned and moving to England. In 1872 his sixth child was born, a son, who died suddenly at the age of seventeen months. In the summer of 1873 he took the whole family to the estate in Samara, but that year a failure of crops produced a famine in the area, and his time was spent in arranging for relief to be brought and contributing to it himself.

He began to write *Anna Karenina* in March 1873. Sonya records in her *Diary* that a neighbor of theirs had given up his mistress — named Anna — for a younger beautiful woman. The rejected mistress committed suicide at the railroad station in Tula by throwing herself under a moving freight train. Tolstoy was present at the autopsy. He felt deeply affected by the circumstances and by the fatal event. In her *Short Autobiography*, Sonya states: "He told me that he wanted to write a novel about the fall of a society woman in the highest Petersburg circles, and the task he set himself was to tell the story of the woman and of her fall without condemning her."

Rarely has a novel that appears to be so much of one piece, so powerfully sustained and so artfully unified, been written with more interruptions and despite so many emotional distractions. In the light of Tolstoy's personal distress, his restlessness and his uncertainties, it is all the more amazing to realize that the novel brought forth under these conditions is magnificent.

At the beginning of the novel, Anna Karenina, who is lovelessly married to a high government official in St. Petersburg, comes to Moscow hoping to improve the situation between her brother Stepan and his wife, Dolly. Anna's brother is a philanderer, and Dolly, having learned of her husband's affairs, is in terrible conflict over whether to separate from him. From the first chapter of the novel until the last, the primary concern in the mind of the author is: *What keeps couples together? What wrenches them apart?*

Stepan's friend, Levin, a wealthy landowner, has come to Moscow at the same time to propose marriage to Dolly's sister, Kitty. While Kitty is attracted to him, she is also flattered by the attention paid her by the dashing Army officer Count Vronsky. She rejects Levin's proposal, but she, in turn, is crushed when Vronsky, fascinated by Mme. Karenina, abandons Kitty to follow Anna back to St. Petersburg.

Through the course of Vronsky's pursuit, Anna recognizes she has never had more than a "marriage of convenience" with her husband, and, in fact, she is as passionately in love with Vronsky as he is with her. While their affair flourishes, Kitty languishes abroad; Levin, alone in his country house, broodingly tries to "cultivate his garden." Stepan and Dolly reconcile themselves to their marriage but at a lower level of integrity.

Levin is clearly the autobiograpical character of the novel. He represents more closely Tolstoy's own view of himself than any other character he had created. Here is a man who exercised his body into athletic excellence, tried to operate his farms with scientific training, opposed the social ideas of the progressives, attempted to cultivate the humanity and the community he sensed among the peasants, and longed to experience and understand the relationship of marriage — all as Tolstoy had done himself. Even his name is closely related. "Levin" is a variation on "Lev," which is "Leo" in Russian.

Eventually Stepan and Dolly bring Levin and Kitty together again, and this time Kitty accepts his proposal. (This courtship and wedding are the artistic expressions of how these events took place between Tolstoy and Sonya.) As they begin their marriage, Anna abandons her life with Karenin and goes abroad to live with Vronsky. But even self-imposed exile is exile, and they do not choose to endure it very long. When they return to Russia they discover that, while the society they belong to condones a secret illicit affair, it will not recognize a woman who publicly rejects her marriage and lives with the man she loves. Cut off from the social life they had been accustomed to, with nowhere else to turn, they retreat to Vronsky's estate in the country, gradually to become even more disheartened. Vronsky is now a man without an occupation who needs contact with public life in order to fulfill himself. Anna, who believes she has no life outside of their love, fears losing him and becomes more possessive — which only makes Vronsky feel that he has no freedom.

In contrast to the steady decay of Anna's situation, Kitty and Levin's marriage grows more secure and significant with the birth of their first child. While they increasingly realize the ideal of family happiness, Anna and Vronsky's relationship becomes more and more difficult. Unable to obtain a divorce from Karenin, Anna is doomed to live as a social outcast and in fear of losing the one value that makes her life worth living — Vronsky's love. The weight of these oppressive conditions eventually overpowers her, and she commits suicide by throwing herself under the wheels of a train.

Anna Karenina has justly been called the greatest novel of society — for it expresses more dramatically than any other single work the power that "social life" has over individual happiness. What gives the novel its great universality is its profound examination of what *social relations* are all about.

Family ties and friendships teach us the conditions of what is acceptable to the society we live in. As we each learn what we want out of life, we also learn "the rules of the game." Of all human relations, love involves us most deeply with another person. Now the institution of marriage makes possible something even better than love alone, namely: the best chance of preserving and enhancing love itself. And one's society — by permitting or prohibiting marriage — determines both the future relations between two people who are in love and the future relations of each of them with the rest of society.

In this respect, *Anna Karenina* is antisociety, because Tolstoy implies that the love between Vronsky and Anna is better than the conventions which make them social exiles. Marriage without love is as bad as love without marriage; but society condones the former and condemns the latter. Society has made its accommodation with the institution of marriage but has lost the spirit of it. What is antisocial in the novel is Tolstoy's condemnation of society's emotional dishonesty, its willingness to prefer appearance to reality. False values make it easy for a whole society to delude itself and live dishonest, superficial lives, just as refusing to be true to oneself enables an individual to live a self-deluding life.

In some respects this may sound old-fashioned. Certainly divorce has become more widespread today than it was a hundred years ago. But "free love" has not. People divorce and remarry, much more often than couples live together without being married. Why is this so? *Anna Karenina* contributes to answering this question because at heart it is concerned with understanding exactly what is the significance of marriage.

It is the implication of *Anna Karenina* that love is the condition which makes one aware of one's best self, and that marriage is the condition that keeps one from becoming a monster of selfishness. This is why marriage is so important. Because it offers the promise of an endless future in which to cultivate as much concern for the other person as for yourself (first your spouse and then your children), it enables you to fulfill yourself, to become your best self. The value this has for society is that, the more fulfilled you are in yourself, the better you are able to participate in society, and vice versa.

This is not to say that marriage is simple or easy. Knowing how hard it is to accommodate to conflicting needs and desires within oneself, it should be obvious how much more difficult it is to maintain harmony between two people — even with the best intentions in the world on the part of each. But without marriage the opportunities to overcome conflicts grow slimmer and slimmer. It is Anna Karenina's tragedy that Vronsky and she are unable to marry. Without that "promise of an endless future," which only society can pretend to guarantee, they are without protection against the conflicts threatening their harmony. Their love is not enough to protect them by itself. They are torn apart by fears for themselves — selfish concerns — that it would have been possible for them to overcome if they had been married.

Being allowed to participate in one's society is as important as the experience of love in order to live a complete life. Anna and Vronsky's love is certainly genuine, but the society they live in destroys them. Society has the power to take its revenge against those who break its rules about marriage. One reason for this may well be that because there is so little genuine love among the majority of people, lovers who break the conventions concerning marriage remind all the others of how shamefully superficial and unfulfilled their own private lives are.

In the end, Vronsky goes off to war. All that his life is good for now is to die for others. But Levin, who rejects the war, experiences a revelation that, out of his family happiness, he is now free to live more simply and directly for the good of others. Somehow this experience of overcoming selfishness is associated with living for God, as well.

Levin's conclusion in *Anna Karenina* leads one out of the novel and back to Tolstoy's own life — for Levin's "revelation" reflects the changes that were taking place in the author's soul by the time he had completed the novel.

In many ways it was a very bad time for Tolstoy. Above all else, he was oppressed by consciousness of death. Between 1873, when he began *Anna Karenina,* and 1877, when he completed it, his seventh, eighth, and ninth children all died in infancy. His beloved Auntie Tatyana, who had been his "second mother," and Aunt Pelageya, his worldly protector during his adolescence in Kazan (who had come to live at Yasnaya Polyana), both died. *Anna Karenina* is permeated with awareness of death, which, after all, is the other side of the author's compassion for the life of each character in the book. What does it mean, ultimately, to be able to feel with others, if we do not also recognize that all life is *threatened* by the extinction of death *at any moment* and *doomed* to the extinction of death *eventually?*

Despite his happiness in achieving the family life he craved, Levin pauses at the open door of his barn and, contemplating the workers at their labor, reflects that:

"They'll bury her, and nothing will be left either of her or of that pretty girl in the red skirt, who with that skillful, soft action shakes the ears out of their husks. They'll bury her and this piebald gelding, and very soon, too," he thought, gazing at the horse heavily breathing through dilated nostrils, its belly rising and falling as it trod the slanting wheel that turned under it. "And they will bury her and Fyodor, who feeds the machine, with his curly beard full of chaff and his shirt torn on his white shoulders — they will bury him. He's untying the sheaves, and giving orders, and shouting to the women, and quickly getting straight the strap on the moving wheel. And what's more, it's not them alone — me they'll bury too, and nothing will be left. What is it all for?"

Tolstoy had reached the farthest point to which his intelligence and imagination could take him as an observer of life, and there he found only one meaningful question: When one recognizes the inevitability of death, how can he go on living?

Begin here

8

Conversion

When a person without food, shelter, clothing, or a job
at which to earn money to buy them *falls into despair,*
we recognize that he is suffering because his basic needs
are not being fulfilled. We think of it as a problem that
can be solved on a practical level. When a person whose
basic needs are fulfilled but whose longing for love,
power, wealth, fame, or prestige is unsatisfied and he
falls into despair, we might consider it the expression of
frustrated ambition and council him to reconcile himself
to what he has and abandon his aspirations or encourage
him to increase efforts toward achieving his desires. But
when a man's needs are fulfilled and his greatest ambi-
tions are satisfied *and still he falls into despair* — how are
we to understand it?

Tolstoy at about age fifty.

At the age of fifty, Count Leo Tolstoy fell into despair — despite the fact that, married to a woman he loved and who had borne him six children who were still alive, he was a man whose chosen literary career had brought him not only the admiration of the critical world but earned him a small fortune as well. He possessed good health, family happiness, fame, and wealth; and still he fell into despair. How is one to understand it?

He asked the question: What is the meaning of life? — and found no answer to satisfy him.

All of the things, the conditions, and the events that are said to give life its value are pursued in vain. Everything passes. Sickness, old age, and death destroy the body. All human relationships are perpetual struggles of love or hate against indifference. Fame is a figment of the imagination. Wealth, power, and prestige are as permanent as a moment of fine weather; they can be blown away in an instant. To find the meaning of life in any or all of these so-called values is the "vanity of vanities." They are all in vain. Conventional ways of life are self-deluded because none of them can give an adequate answer to *why* one should live at all, when death will ultimately destroy every life.

Such a line of reasoning led Tolstoy to the verge of suicide.

One way to understand why this came about is to remember how Tolstoy had always pursued the idea of self-perfection. His program was to do everything possible for the betterment of whatever he concerned himself with. Consider, for example, his concern with his body. Most people are willing to let their bodies mature and decay without ever realizing the potentialities of its structure or its organism. It goes "soft" from lack of development. Without cultivated definition, without differentiation, muscles and fat merge into each other. But the athletic development of the body means that distinctions are cultivated and the potential differences accentuated in order to bring out the fullest possibilities of their special powers. Such cultivation of the body's musculature is called *articulation*: giving the best possible shape to the muscles, making explicit what is only implicit in their nature, making specific what is otherwise vague. "Articulation" is a word that comes from description of speech. It means that speech is correctly practiced only when the power to speak is fully developed so that sounds are clear and words properly enunciated.

A writer is one who tries in words to make clear, specific, and distinct what he experiences in life. He uses words to give a more exact shape to experience. He uses language to articulate what is otherwise only formless or vague.

It is reasonable to think of Tolstoy's career as a continual process of self-perfection in the sense that he tried to articulate first his body and his mind, then his personal life, his professional position, and ultimately his soul. This is the basis of his art. It is the essence of his powers of expression in the service of truth.

In his own spirit, as his writings reflect, he articulated his experiences of childhood, and his encounters with nature, with people of a different culture, and with incidents of personal life, as he also articulated his experiences with war and with education. His great novels articulate the character of individual, social, and political life. Their realism is incomparably effective — not because his ideas are always irrefutable — but because his expression of human experiences is always true to life. Most people recognize that what is being made explicit is something they have experienced themselves but not articulated.

There is nothing deranged in Tolstoy's despair. The reason his expression of it is not a pathological case study, but rather an appeal from his soul to the souls of all the thousands of readers who have been affected by it, lies in the fact that he articulates the muscles of his spirit whereas others are willing to let them go soft for lack of development. What he expresses is as universal as the experience of childhood or romantic love or war. It is the condition of human life to ask: Wherein are values to be found? Knowing that death is ever-present and that all things change, what should I do to make life worth living? How am I to understand the meaning of life? When a man is not able to push these questions to the back of his mind but allows them to dominate the forefront of his thought, then he is confronted by such a crisis as overcame Tolstoy in the middle of his life.

The record of that crisis for Tolstoy is to be found in his slim book called *A Confession*. It marks his turning away, by the end of the 1870's, from the life he had lived up to that time. He had been a man of the world, an artist, and an intellectual. But he had found no satisfactory answers to the questions of how to live. He turned to religion. He turned from the love of himself, as he understood that now, to the love of God — and such a turning is what is meant by the word "conversion."

In simplicity and sincerity, *A Confession* records the trials he went through to the point of understanding he had achieved shortly after the completion of *Anna Karenina*. It traces his argument that neither science nor philosophy is able to give or is interested in giving significant answers to the questions. Considering how the members of his own class lived, he found that those who choose ignorance, for lack of talent to think clearly or out of fear, live only for their pleasure, while those who see the question and find no answer either kill themselves or live in cynical self-contempt. He considered himself a member of the latter group. But the very fact that he continued to live gave him reason to suppose he might have overlooked some other source of understanding.

If the members of his social class had lost the meaning of life, lived only for their idle pleasures and dreaded the approach of death, how was it that peasants, whose life

of work seemed nothing but a burden to the privileged,
appeared to find life meaningful? What gave their lives
meaning was their simple faith in God. Tolstoy sought
out pilgrims, monks, unlettered laborers. He visited monasteries to talk with the elders. He remained repelled by
what he took to be the superstitious folderol of the
Church, but one fact seemed inescapable to him. Peasants
who lived in the faith approached death with tranquility,
not with the suffering or the selfish greed for life that he
saw in everyone else. Tolstoy came to believe that the
peasants' faith in God gave their lives meaning that death
does not destroy, and that this is *the purpose of all religions* — a goal which cannot be apprehended by reason.

Appreciating this aspect of peasant life — "How often
I envied the peasants their illiteracy and lack of learning!" he wrote — Tolstoy set out to become a church
member, a participant in the rituals and rites of the Greek
Orthodox Church. It was the religious community of his
childhood, the only recognized religious order of the nation in which he lived. This lasted for three years, until
he could no longer blind himself to the contradictions he
found. After that he left the Church permanently.

A Confession then records two movements. One is the
conversion to religious faith; the other is the rejection of
the Church. It was one thing for Tolstoy to find that life
becomes meaningful through the humility, mercifulness,
brotherly love, labor, and renunciation of a life of pleasures which follow from the love of God. But it is quite

another thing to recognize that each Church considers its "prescriptions" for salvation exclusive to its members and therefore condemns all others; to consider the elaborations of Christian theology loaded with nonsense and to be offended by a whole host of propositions which cannot be supported either by common sense or by reason; to face the fact that, as far as national law and international affairs are concerned, the Church is a functioning arm of the state, supporting its policies of violence and murder.

Tolstoy sought a way to make life meaningful. He believed he had found the key in the faith simple people have in God and most particularly through the teachings of Jesus. He attempted to act on such faith by belonging to the Church that calls itself Christian. But he found that interwoven with the moral ideals expounded by Jesus were totally contradictory tenets of the Church, which, as an institution, it held just as firmly as if they were at the heart of the religion. *A Confession* ends with the following promise:

> That there is truth in the teaching is to me indubitable but it is also certain that there is falsehood in it, and I must find what is true and what is false, must disentangle the one from the other. I am setting to work upon this task.

With that program in mind, Tolstoy initiated the second career of his long lifetime. Out of his own needs — just as he had become a literary artist thirty years before — now, hardly anticipating how it would shape the remaining thirty years of his life, he became a religious reformer.

Between 1879 and 1881 Tolstoy made his greatest effort at a systematic examination of the teachings of the Church in relation to the original four gospels on which they are based. He wrote with the passion of an explorer recounting his discovery of "A New World" and in the hope of directing others to voyage to it, despite the fact that he knew these writings might never be published in Russia. Inasmuch as they were critical of the established Church, government censorship would not sanction their appearance, and, as he expected, they were not made available — except in clandestine editions — until many years after they were written.

The first of these books is called *An Examination of Dogmatic Theology*. Fulfilling his promise at the end of *A Confession,* it is an extraordinarily courageous attack on the ways in which the Church teachings have corrupted and abused what Jesus himself had taught. Tolstoy rejected all that seemed meaninglessly mystifying and conflicting with what he took to be the essence of Christ's moral teachings. At the hub of everything he found The Sermon on the Mount, and from it he abstracted five principles or commandments, which he presented as the crux of the religious orientation that makes life intrinsically meaningful. They can be summarized in the following way:

1. Do not be angry.

2. Do not lust.
3. Do not swear oaths.
4. Resist not him that is evil.
5. Love your enemies.

Anger, lust, and swearing allegiance to someone else are all means of subjecting oneself to conditions that destroy human brotherhood and debase oneself. To refuse to resist evil is the negative way toward good, for it means that you do not contribute to evil yourself. This — in the long run — has proved to be the most significant of Tolstoy's teachings, for it has been the basis for all the important nonviolent political resistance movements of the past century. It flows through the preaching and actions of Gandhi in India a generation ago as it does today in the civil rights movement led by Martin Luther King Jr. in the United States. It does not mean that one should accept evil; it means, rather, that one should not use violence against violence or evil against evil. And to love your enemy — to love *even* your enemy — is to see beyond the conditions that separate one man from another to the‘humanity that joins one with another. If one is able to act according to these precepts, then one's life is essentially worthwhile by virtue of what it is, not for what may come of it.

The second work was called *Union and Translation of the Four Gospels.* Tolstoy offered the Greek, the standard Russian translation, and his own version in parallel columns. By reorganizing the material he presented his own version of Jesus' life and thought. Distilled through his filters of reason and conscience, the story as Tolstoy tells it is without concern for definitions of the nature of God or worries over the creation of the world or the meaning of redemption. Salvation as he understood it is primarily moral. To be "saved" is to find the conditions that make life worth living. The rest is distraction; for the poetry and the window dressing of church dogma only removes man from religion by placing the so-called ideals of the Church so far out of reach of the ordinary man that he imagines religion is something one performs in certain ceremonies or gives lip service to — something that has no connection with his daily life.

The column that presented Tolstoy's interpretation of the life of Jesus was subsequently printed separately and has come to be widely known as *A Short Account of the Gospels.*

In 1881 Czar Alexander II was murdered by terrorists among the revolutionists, and Tolstoy proposed, in a letter addressed to Alexander III, that to pardon those who were responsible for his father's death would be a far more valuable action than the revenge of execution. His letter was never delivered. But the approach in this instance became the formula for much of Tolstoy's later social and political criticism. It is the absence of moral ideals that makes public as well as private life the misery of perpetuating the return of evil for evil.

Tolstoy was a gigantically respected personality. The

sincerity with which he turned to religion was soon talked about among his personal acquaintances and among those who live merely on hearsay about the great — but it was considered an eccentric abberation. Indeed, Dostoevsky (who never met Tolstoy but admired him and felt in sympathy with him) relayed the rumor in a letter to his wife that in St. Petersburg at that time people were saying: ". . . Tolstoy has almost lost his mind and perhaps may have gone completely insane."

Out of his own longing to overcome conflict with those he knew, Tolstoy wrote a letter of apology to Turgenev to breach the gap in their friendship after seventeen years. Although they had several amiable meetings after that, the atheist Turgenev never comprehended the reasons for or the significance of Tolstoy's conversion.

It was even less comprehensible to the people closest to him: his wife and his children. There is nothing so distressing to those who give conventional lip service to religion as the presence of one who takes it seriously. During this same period, Sonya gave birth to their tenth child in 1879 and their eleventh in 1881. Their financial affairs were complicated by Tolstoy's neglect of the family estate, as well as the property far away in Samara. The responsibility for managing these fell to Sonya, who handled it with difficulty and against her will, but with fear for the future of the family. The first effect of Tolstoy's putting his soul in order was to place his family happiness in danger.

9

The Family Tragedy

Precisely at the time when Tolstoy wished to begin to simplify his life, his family's needs required that he make it even more complex — that is, Sonya's view of what the family needed. They had lived in the country for nearly twenty years. Now Countess Tolstoy insisted that they spend most of each year in Moscow. Their eldest son must enter the university, the next two sons were to begin at the gymnasium, and their eldest daughter must enroll in art school. They rented a large house and were no sooner installed than they found themselves in an atmosphere crowded with callers and invitations, visited by relatives and friends, the distinguished and the hangers-on, to say nothing of the hordes of playmates of all their children. They were wealthy, and they lived in the manner to which their class was accustomed. The heartlessness of the big city, with its excesses of time-killing and soul-numbing distractions, had always distressed Tolstoy. But now that he wished to live a more significant life it seemed more than paradoxical, it seemed almost a deliberate affront, that he was called upon to live less significantly. The fact that he felt so "called upon," and that he answered this "call" of Sonya's to the extent that he did, determined the pattern of their personal life for his remaining years.

He was torn between supporting the way of life that was necessary for his wife and establishing a new life for himself.

He felt a tremendous guilt — a guilt he must take on personally — when he was struck by the incredible contrast in Moscow between the luxury of the life of the rich and the misery of the life of the poor. It was not that he had never been conscious of poverty before (as Sonya bitingly accused him). But, through his new belief in the responsibility each man should feel for another, he apprehended the existence of the thousands of miserable sufferers in a way that affected him as it never had before. How could he go on living the life of the idle rich, seated at a banquet every evening, served by dozens of white-gloved waiters and butlers, when he knew, felt, suffered the fact that thousands were starving to death, freezing to death, rotting with disease? He experienced this with as much intensity as a man who suddenly looked down at his own body and found it covered with maggots eating him alive.

There was his responsibility to his wife and family on the one hand and his suffering for humanity on the other. If he gave away all of his fortune in little amounts to every victim of poverty in Moscow, what would he accomplish? He would bring his family to destitution for the rest of their lives while helping the poor over one or two days. The solution did not seem to lie in giving away his money. But to help both the poor and the rich to see better what the meaning of life is and what everyone's responsibility is — that made sense to him. He began work on a book to be called *What Then Must We Do?*

Under these conditions, it is easy to see why conflict with his wife intensified. After an argument during the summer of 1882 in the country, Sonya wrote in her diary:

. . . For the first time in my life Lyovochka has run away from me and is spending the night in his study. We quarreled over trifles. I attacked him for not troubling himself over the children, for not attending to Ilya who is sick, and for not making their jackets. But it is not a matter of jackets, the matter is that he is growing cold toward me and the children. Today he loudly shouted that his most passionate desire is to get away from the family.

To make it up to her, after that, he bought a house in Moscow, repaired it, furnished it from top to bottom, and had it all ready for her on her arrival in the fall. It was a grand gesture she could not appreciate. For a woman who is fearful that her husband can "do without her" it is no pleasure to see him manage completely on his own household affairs which until then had been entirely her responsibility.

Tolstoy undertook to learn Hebrew from a rabbi in Moscow in order to pursue his study of the *Old Testament*. Sonya found this no more to her taste than the time he had invested in learning Greek. What had become of the author she had married? — the man who wrote the short stories, plays, and novels she had adored copying? Their separations grew longer. In the spring of 1883 Tolstoy set out for his estate in Samara, and, while they corresponded as they always had (even if they were separated for only twenty-four hours) with more than one letter a day, they remained apart now for three months. During that time he sent her the draft of his book *What I Believe* and, in reply, he received the following remarks summing up Sonya's position — from which she was to remain unmoved:

> . . . Of course, it is impossible to say anything against your idea that it would be fine for people to be perfect, and undoubtedly one must remind people that it is necessary to be perfect and what paths they must follow to achieve perfection. Yet I can scarcely refrain from saying that it is *hard* to give up all the toys of life with which one plays, and everyone — and I more than others — keeps a firm grasp on

these playthings, and rejoices in the way they glitter, make noise, and amuse. . . .

Their attitudes were irreconcilable. The demands of social life were at war with the demands of a spiritual life. But now Tolstoy was aware that he might lose Sonya's love, a fear as new to him as the fear of losing his love was old for her. From then on, each out of his own needs tried to keep alive the love of the other — without giving up his or her own principles. It was a seesaw movement throughout their remaining years.

Still the essence of Tolstoy's religious insight is that salvation — finding life worth living — lies in seeking not one's personal welfare but social welfare, and a man's family is his most important social experience. He wished that his wife and children might be entirely in sympathy with his ideas, but he would not be justified in turning his back on them even if they were in opposition to the ideas. Sonya's resistance rested on a variety of reasons. She was not interested in the analysis of ethics, to say nothing of theological problems; she was convinced that the censors would not allow any kind of criticism of the Church to be published in Russia; she was fearful of social disapproval; and she knew that such books as *What I Believe* could not earn nearly the amounts of money Tolstoy's fiction had brought them.

It was fiction that Sonya wanted him to return to. Not that he had entirely given up story writing for "preaching." During the same year that he finished *What I Be-*

lieve, Tolstoy produced the stories *What Men Live By* for a children's magazine and started on the superb novella called *The Death of Ivan Ilyich.* But he had not yet worked out his own ideas of what the relationship ought to be between art and a moral life. He began to make notes on his thoughts about the question at this time; it is these which several years later developed into his challenging study *What Is Art?*

In the fall of the year, Tolstoy met V. G. Chertkov, a man of twenty-nine, who appeared to be the image of Tolstoy's soul. Aristocratic, well-educated, independent-minded, he had voluntarily abandoned his position as an officer in the Czar's Guards to devote himself to the welfare of the peasants on his large estate. The study of the Gospels and particularly his understanding of Jesus' teachings had led him to believe in humility, productive work, and the abandonment of luxury. He was unmarried, righteous, and hard-working. In him, Tolstoy found his most devout disciple. In Tolstoy, Chertkov found his Master. And Sonya found the embodiment of her natural enemy — the man she came to think of as an "evil genius."

With the beginning of 1884 Tolstoy's writings started to attract to him *followers* in the sense of would-be believers looking for a teacher who could point the way for them. Through correspondence and by visits from people unknown to him who simply appeared at Tolstoy's home, he became aware that his ideas were initiating a "movement." For such followers, the problem of how to live according to the commandments of Jesus, was to be solved by becoming *Tolstoyans*. These followers, who increased in numbers every year, were the bane of Sonya's existence. She called them "the dark people"; they hovered over her life like vultures. The tension between her conflicts with her husband and the knowledge that he was coming to be considered a *religious leader* contributed to the growing hysteria in her life.

While he was determined not to abandon his family, Tolstoy could not do otherwise than attempt to persuade them of his beliefs — not through preaching but by example. He humbled himself by hard physical labor, and he practiced what he preached about productive work. He learned from a craftsman how to make boots; he did all the menial work of caring for himself — he swept the floor, emptied the chamber pot, and mended his clothes — he pumped the water for the household and transported it in huge tubs; he worked in the fields, plowing, mowing, lugging manure, felling trees, carting timber, and carpentering. For a while these actions had a remarkable effect on the family. During their summers at Yasnaya Polyana, the three eldest sons worked in the fields with their father; even Sonya and the girls spent some of the time with them. But numerous conditions irritated the Countess. The "pilgrims" who sought out her husband were bad enough. The fact that he rejected his title, refusing to be called "Count" any longer; refused to swear an oath and was fined for not serving on jury duty; decided henceforth not to eat meat — all of this distressed her. The final irritation, which drove her to thoughts of suicide, was to find herself pregnant again, at forty years of age, and to give birth to a child in 1884.

Chertkov's presence continued to threaten Sonya with the fear that, if Tolstoy ever fell fully "into his clutches," he would abandon the family. Tolstoy, however, could not see enough of the young disciple. Chertkov could be stuffy and holier-than-thou, and he debated with Tolstoy sometimes with arrogant self-righteousness. But, such nastiness aside, the two men found each other invaluable. Chertkov was, above all else, Tolstoy's strongest ally in his relations with the outside world. He had considerable charm as well as ability as an organizer and financial manager. In response to Tolstoy's suggestion that good literature should be made available to the masses through inexpensive editions, Chertkov arranged for the establishment of the *Intermediary,* which pioneered the business of cheap market paperbacks. In the first four years they sold twelve million copies. Tolstoy contributed tales similar to those in *What Men Live By,* and the remainder of the list included works of Charles Dickens, George Eliot, and Matthew Arnold, among others.

Out of this arrangement, begun innocently enough, developed the most concrete issue over which Sonya came to battle against Chertkov, namely: Who would publish Tolstoy's writings in the future? At the beginning of 1885 Sonya had Tolstoy's agreement for her to republish all of his writings prior to 1881. This venture alone assured her of a considerable annual income. But Chertkov's request for the rights to certain works for his own publishing purposes in the *Intermediary* made the disagreement between the two of them hostile and undisguised. When Tolstoy wrote him of the suffering he endured in his own "insane, immoral" household, Chertkov did not hesitate to advise him to leave it all behind him. But then suddenly Tolstoy's two eldest daughters decided to become "Tolstoyans" themselves, and there was, at least for a little while, a source of comfort within the family — the kind that Tolstoy had longed for and little expected.

Sonya, however, remained adamant about the education of the children and the rounds of social life to which she was accustomed and determined to maintain, which meant living most of the year in Moscow. "Moral perfection I will never attain. . . ." she once wrote. "And I cannot enjoy material pleasures because some discerning and stern critic always appears and plunges me into despair at once. That is why I do not love life." The threat of leaving each other came more often and with less control. Tolstoy raged about getting a divorce. Sonya packed her trunks and swore she would never return. Each one thought the other morbidly, emotionally unbalanced if not clinically insane. Neither one understood how it was possible that the other did not appreciate the anguish he suffered. Each one wanted to go on living with the other — but only on his own terms. Neither one got what he wanted.

10

The Kingdom of God

The family tragedy itself was a result of Tolstoy's determination to live in the world as it is and to realize his conception of goodness there. During the following years numerous attempts were made by his followers to lure him away from his family into a life in some "ideal community." Such Tolstoyan communities were actually begun during the next few decades not only in Russia but in England, Holland, and various parts of the United States. Tolstoy refused to participate in them — except to give advice. He argued that more important than cultivating the escapist, hothouse atmosphere of monasteries or nunneries is the effort to remain in the tangle of actual circumstances in which one finds himself and to fulfill the ideal of "The Kingdom of God" there.

At the beginning of 1886, Tolstoy's son Alyosha died. He was four years old. His death did not strike his father as painfully as the deaths of his other children had. He now had a sense of unity with nature, of identity with the moral purposes of life, which enabled him at the age of fifty-eight to suffer such a loss without the egocentric sorrows of a man without faith. It was his faith that swept him along now with the sense of being a prophet — one whose work is in the here and now but whose value is to be measured only by eternity.

Tolstoy completed *What Then Must We Do?* It is not merely an exposé of poverty in Russia. It is a moral indictment of the economic conditions of a society enabling one class of people to exploit all other classes because of the laws of property and the nature of money. For want of a solution to the problems created by the unequal distribution of property and the unfair power of money, Tolstoy predicted (in 1886) that "a workers' revolution with horrors of destruction and murder" would occur. In that year Lenin was sixteen years old; Trotsky and Stalin were each only seven years old. In that year balls and dinner parties in Moscow dominated the social life of Tolstoy's family, and the unforgivable absurdity of living off the labor of others gave him no peace of mind.

He was then the most famous author *unpublished* in Russia. All of his writings on religion were prohibited from being printed in his own country. They became known, circulated, sold, and copied by admirers only stealthily and illegally. While his reputation grew and the effect of his thought influenced an always increasing number of people, his stature as a dangerous foe of the Church and the government rose. The police kept him under constant surveillance. Only his importance as an internationally renowned figure saved him from jail or worse; but it did not save his admirers. To the end of his life, Tolstoy was never personally persecuted by the authorities, although his followers were increasingly humiliated, harried, arrested, exiled, or executed.

During the summer of that year a leg infection caused a severe illness, which kept Tolstoy in bed for more than two months. He worked at an incredible pace on new literary projects. Not only did he write a slight comedy as temperance propaganda, called *The First Distiller,* but he also finished both *The Death of Ivan Ilyich* and the play *The Power of Darkness.*

The Death of Ivan Ilyich sounds the perfectly clear message that one who lives merely by the standards of the world will die by them — hollow and unfulfilled. Ivan Ilyich is a man who had never known what he lived for, other than to achieve the surface appearances of success. And the approach of death enabled even such a self-deceiving man to see them for the superficialities that they are. What makes the story the overwhelming experience it is is the compassion with which Tolstoy treats the hero, the sufferer who can hardly grasp what has happened to him. The implication of the tale is inescapable. Why do men live such pointless, empty lives? The over-all effect of the novella is to make each reader face himself with the question: Is my own life any more significant? any more intrinsically worthwhile? Ivan Ilyich is the "Everyman" of ordinary bourgeois society, nobody's fool, no failure in the eyes of the world. But the certainty of his death makes him as pathetic as a martyr would be if he did not know what cause he died for. Life without salvation is as unfair as the torture of innocent hostages, for Ivan Ilyich has no conception — no elevating, justifying idea — in the light of which he can understand why he has lived at all, until it is too late. From a literary point of view, *The Death of Ivan Ilyich* is one of the most profoundly moving, brilliant pieces of writing of all time. It is a masterpiece of world literature.

By itself that greatly pleased Sonya — Tolstoy had returned to creative writing — to say nothing of the pleasure it brought her to feel needed by him during his illness. But the play, *The Power of Darkness,* created other problems. It is a grim study of the dark side of peasant life, cramped and distorted by moral as well as intellectual ignorance, destroyed by passionate drives and uncontrolled lust. Tolstoy was no innocent, imagining that the peasant was a "noble savage" whose life was all admirable simplicity. The play was not a closet drama; the author hoped to see it performed on the stage. It was read to the Czar, who was moved and gave his approval for a production — until he was influenced by the Procurator of the Holy Synod (the government's official "protector" of the Church) to change his mind and prohibit its performance. He declared that the play was an "offense against taste" and "debasing." There was no indication that the play misrepresented the life of peasants but rather that it was "too realistic and frightful." Royal opinion in this case is typical of the attitude that kept the Czar personally and the government in general from the demands made upon them to "face facts." They were incapable of recognizing hard truths. But the play was soon translated and circulated abroad. It was first staged in 1888 in Paris, where Émile Zola helped to arrange for the production.

In the meanwhile visitors continued to call on Tolstoy from all over Europe and even the United States: the highly educated as well as the plainest sorts of people, the talented and the half mad. A young philosopher named Masaryk was one such visitor. He was to become the first president of Czechoslovakia. Writers such as Leskov and Romain Rolland came to see him. Journalists interviewed him. Chertkov, now married and the father of a child, took up much of Tolstoy's time during this period when he was hard at work on his next attempt to express better and more fully "what he believed." This became the book entitled *On Life*. It remains one of Tolstoy's least read works, probably because it is an exceedingly abstract, tightly argued, philosophic tract almost devoid of the story-teller's art which attracts most readers to him. But it is powerfully clear, earnest, and challenging; a work of sustained and systematic reasoning that organizes all of the general principles of Tolstoy's position and lays the foundations for his future works of social criticism.

By 1888, at the age of sixty, the pattern of Tolstoy's life was of long days filled with hard physical labor, long hours of concentrated thinking and writing, lengthy correspondence with friends and "unknowns," and conversations with those who asked for his advice in one regard or another. By this time he had given up alcohol, meat, and tobacco. He wrote vividly not only against the cruelty of slaughterhouses in his arguments for vegetarianism, but he also wrote a remarkable esasy, *Why Do Men Stupefy Themselves?,* explaining that the desire to "blind" and "dope" oneself daily with drinking and smoking expresses the need to escape from a guilty conscience — in other words, to escape from our inability to face life honestly, which alone would enable man to live morally.

In 1889 Tolstoy published a work that became a scandalous success and caused him anguish, for all his willingness to stand by it. This was the novella named after a work by Beethoven, *The Kreutzer Sonata,* although it is much less about the effects of music than it is about the effects of sexual passion. Passionate love in this story leads to jealousy and murder. What it proposes is chastity even between a husband and wife except for the purpose of producing children. Why did the book bring scorn

Tolstoy in his study at Yasnaya Polyana.

to the author? First of all, to write about sexual passion was considered improper to begin with. Prudish people condemned it for what appeared to be its subject matter, Libertines, on the other hand, made fun of it in contrast to the earlier fiction of the same author — for the Tolstoy of *Anna Karenina* and many shorter works understood only too well the compelling power of sexual passion. But Tolstoy's purpose here is to make a point about the moral justification of sexuality; to set up an awareness of the ideal it realizes and bring the reader to acknowledge that anything short of that ideal is immoral regardless of whatever other ideas explain the alternatives. What the literary critics and the general public had to struggle with (and, since they were unable to adjust to the idea, they misinterpreted the work) was the fact that Tolstoy was writing here more as a Biblical moralist or philosopher of ethics than as a realistic novelist or "reporter." In a certain sense, people are more sensitive to any criticism of their sexual behavior than they are to being reminded of their lack of true religion. However, the unpleasant aftereffects of that publication blew away in the steady wind of new concerns that constantly occupied the aging author.

No longer able to spend as much physical effort in hard labor, Tolstoy now worked with his daughters in the school for peasants' children; he campaigned against a new anti-Semitic law; he found almost any appeal to help the poor or oppressed impossible to refuse. In the fall of

1891 all of his ingenuity and strength were called upon to act in aid of the starving population, for throughout southeastern Russia a famine threatened millions of peasants with death.

There was no organized attempt on the part of the government to ease the crisis. As a matter of fact, the Czar, the court, and the official newspapers acted as if the famine did not exist. Conventional philanthropy by which the rich dole out assistance to the poor had always revolted Tolstoy for the shame that it concealed — the fact that the rich possess their excess of means by having abused the poor. But in this case, since there was no forthright governmental attempt to alleviate the situation, Tolstoy found himself swept up in the movement to enlist the aid of the rich (both Russian and foreign) who gave money, food, clothing, medicine, time, and energy to travel to the suffering area and work for the relief of the victims.

Tolstoy himself made many inspection tours, wrote articles of appeal, helped to organize the distribution of goods, set up food kitchens — all of which preoccupied him for the better part of two years. Tens of thousands were helped in this way, and Tolstoy's actions endeared him to the Russian people as nothing else he had done. It sharpened the fact that on the international scene he had become "the conscience of mankind."

Scourging the government for its indifference to the starving masses accentuated his arguments for the general conditions by which the idle live on the labor of others. He proclaimed that the need to help the oppressed is not a matter of occasional relief work but ought to be a personal obligation of everyone at all times. Entirely unable to understand Tolstoy's criticism of both the aetheistic revolutionists and the Church, the government branded him an "unbridled" socialist.

He could no longer abide the burden of his wealth in a world of crushing poverty. Nor could he inflict suffering on his family by giving away his worldly goods to others. The way out of the conflict he chose was the technical compromise of legally divesting himself of his properties by willing them to his wife and children as if he were already dead. The transfer of rights became official in the fall of 1892. At that time his possessions were worth about half a million dollars. He was free of ownership — but not of other responsibilities toward his family. The problems of management which this transfer of rights gave Sonya weighed heavily on her, and she never forgave him or let him forget.

These years of action and reflection reached their height in the publication of Tolstoy's book *The Kingdom of God Is Within You*. Prohibited in Russia, with the statement by the censor that "this is the most harmful of all books that he had ever had occasion to ban," it was printed first in France in 1893. Tolstoy here fully develops his religious anarchy.

Against the Church he argues that all so-called Christian institutions have corrupted, disguised, and perverted Jesus' teaching. They have made it into a religion of personal salvation and, as merely a "dessert" of afterlife reward, separated it from its significance for daily living. Having lost or hidden the meaning of Christ's social doctrines, churches function merely to support the immoral nature of national governments.

Against governments, Tolstoy took the stand of the moralist who sees that their existence debases and oppresses the lives of the great majority for the useless lives of the elite. In order to maintain the advantages of the rich and powerful, governments systematically brutalize all others by the use of force — in collecting taxes, perpetuating prisons, and waging wars.

But Christ's teaching is that salvation — the Kingdom of God — is not to be achieved except in one's own life, here and now, and only by recognizing that each person's life

> . . . does not belong to himself or his family or the State but to Him who sent him into the world, and that he must therefore fulfill not the law of his personality or family or State, but the infinite law of Him from Whom he has come — and he will feel himself absolutely free from all human authorities and will even cease to regard them as able to trammel anyone.

In order to free himself from *all human authority*, Tolstoy proposes that man refuse to serve the government in any way: refuse to swear oaths, pay taxes, or serve in the army. He calls for outlawing war, for abolishing private property, for maintaining universal peace, and for facilitating the economic self-sufficiency of the masses. Insofar as commitment to these ends would bring one into direct conflict with governments, the essential Christian doctrine or nonresistance to evil means nonviolent resistance. In sum, *The Kingdom of God Is Within You* stands as the world's greatest single work of religious anarchy, Tolstoy's magnificent plea for and justification of civil disobedience. It is the climax of his lifetime search for "the secret written on the Green Stick" — the game he had played with Nikolai in childhood. It contains the essence of his thought as a religious and social reformer. With majestic scorn for all evil and the shams that decorate it, Tolstoy sweeps away the pretenses of the two major obstacles to individual life — the Church and the State — in order to concentrate on the one truth of importance, of value in itself: what makes one's own life worth living.

I I

At the Turn of the Century

Czar Alexander III died in November 1894, and his son became Nicholas II. For a brief moment, as preparations for his coronation were being made, there was a flurry of hope that he might grant the country the constitution it needed or at least initiate some of the reforms that could have made things better. Instead, Nicholas reaffirmed all of the reactionary traditions of the political tyranny he had inherited. Doomed by the same incapacity to see the necessity for change which had blinded his predecessors, it was his fate to become the last of all the Czars. Along with his wife and their five children, he was executed by the Communists in 1918. At the occasion of the coronation Tolstoy remarked in his diary that the "insanity and baseness" of the situation under the new order remains

Nicholas II, Czar of Russia. (1894-1917).

the same as under the old.

Early in 1895 quarrels between the Tolstoys reached a new pitch of hysteria. Tolstoy repudiated royalties on all of his writings published after his conversion (after 1881) but much of Sonya's income for the family was derived from her publication of his earlier works. The latest dispute occurred because Tolstoy sent a new story of his, *Master and Man,* to the editor of a magazine, whereas Sonya wanted to have "first rights" to it for her series. One night after an argument of gruesome intensity, Sonya ran out into the street, in freezing weather, dressed only in slippers and a bathrobe. Tolstoy threw on his clothes and followed her. On the snow-covered streets he begged her to come back. At first she screamed that she would rather be taken to an insane asylum or a jail, but she was finally persuaded to return home with him. The next day the scene occurred again. She was determined to lose herself in the woods on the hills outside the city and freeze to death. It was their daughter Masha who brought her home. Two days later she attempted it again but was restrained by the children. Tolstoy withdrew the story from the magazine. Sonya had it for her edition. Calm descended on the household.

Within a few days of these events, the family was united by the grief they all experienced at the death of the youngest child, Ivan, who was killed by scarlet fever at the age of seven. He was Sonya's baby, her last child, and both parents considered him the most promising of all their offspring. He had a more understanding, joyous, and loving nature than any of their other children. Both parents were crushed, Sonya for the loss of the child who was her greatest consolation, Tolstoy for the belief that the one child would have truly carried on his work was lost.

In time, other family events carried them along. Ilya, who had married the year before, presented them with a grandchild. Now Sergei, their eldest son, took a wife, and soon afterward their two oldest daughters married. Births,

Gorki and Tolstoy.

THE BETTMANN ARCHIVE

marriages, and deaths marked the years. Some of the winter was spent in Moscow. Otherwise they remained at Yasnaya, where relatives, friends, and admirers visited them.

The social worker Jane Addams came from the United States; the psychiatrist Lombroso came from Italy; the poet Rilke from Germany. Pianists and painters stayed with them. Among the new Russian authors, both Gorki and Chekhov were warmly welcomed, and they returned more than once. Tolstoy continued to read voraciously.

Chekhov and Tolstoy.

BROWN BROTHERS

Not only did he keep up with contemporary literature, even writing introductions to the works of some young writers (such as Guy de Maupassant) but he studied a wide range of Oriental thought — Confuscius, Lao-tze, and Buddha, especially — and reread classic authors such as Goethe and Rousseau. His library at Yasnaya Polyana alone grew to number nearly fifteen thousand books.

His own literary projects continued to be numerous. In this period he began the novels *Resurrection* and *Hadji Murad,* as well as the plays *The Light Shineth in Darkness* and *The Live Corpse.* Most of these remained incomplete until he had finished *What Is Art?,* which appeared in 1897. This was some fifteen years after he had started making notes toward a theory of art. It contains a remarkable review of all the significant literature on aesthetics from the middle of the eighteenth century, when the German philosopher Baumgarten coined the word, to the end of the nineteenth century. It then goes on to make Tolstoy's original contribution.

Art is a human activity and therefore has a conscious intention. Despite those who answer that the purpose is "the creation of beauty," no two philosophers of art agree on what is meant by "beauty," for it is experienced only subjectively. No objective criterion for it has been established. But if one starts afresh and asks what art *does,* then, Tolstoy proposes, one will discover that it *transmits or communicates feelings.* The feelings of a (real or imagined) experience are handed on by the artist to the audience so that they too may be "infected" by the qualities of the experience. But what is the end or goal achieved thereby?

> Art is not . . . the manifestation of some mysterious idea of beauty or God; it is not . . . a game in which man lets off his excess of stored-up energy; it is not the expression of man's emotions by external signs; it is not the production of pleasing objects; and, above all, it is not pleasure; but it is a means of union among men joining them together in the same feelings, and indispensable for the life and progress toward well-being of individuals and of humanity.

The means of art is contagiousness or infectiousness of feeling, and this depends upon the sincerity of the artist. Its goal is the progressive unity of mankind in brotherhood. Implicit in this idea is not only a standard for determining whether a work is genuine art or a counterfeit but also the degrees to which a work of art is good. Tolstoy was most concerned about the relationships between art and morality, and his conclusion is that what is best in art is identical with what is best in religion.

Tolstoy received an enormous amount of criticism for *What Is Art?* He himself was never thoroughly satisfied with it, feeling that something of the "mysterious and important" nature of art is not captured by his theory. Nevertheless, it has withstood most of the attacks on it. His idea of "infectiousness" of feeling has been given a new life in twentieth-century aesthetics through the idea of "empathy" — a word, referring to the audience feeling what the characters in a work of art feel, *as if* they too were human beings. Empathy with a work of art, then, is the equivalent of sympathy with a living person: the experience of feeling what the other feels. Compassion is the key to all human values.

At the age of seventy Tolstoy was busy with articles as well as a new novel. He wrote about the public issues of the day, about religion and reason, about political problems. The Americans were at war with Spain; England was at war with the South Africans. International peace conferences were organized. Tolstoy considered them frauds. The power to end war is not possible in governments (which live by violence), he argued, but in the hands of individuals who fight wars. If individuals refuse to serve in armies, wars will cease. Patriotism came in for Tolstoy's knife-sharp criticism as he interpreted the artificial "pumping up" of good feeling between the French and the Russians (when representatives of their armed forces visited each other's country) as a fake use of "brotherhood" to prepare for criminal "alliances" in the event of a world war.

Tolstoy studied Marx and other philosophers who proposed revolutionary means for radical improvements. His inevitable conclusion was:

Even if that should happen which Marx predicted, then the only thing that will happen is that despotism will be passed on. Now the capitalists are ruling, but then the directors of the working class will rule.

Tolstoy never failed to contend that economic conditions do not alter individual consciousness but, rather, the life of humanity is progressively improved only by living according to religious principles.

Socialism will never destroy poverty and the injustice of inequality of capacities. Justice and equality in the good things of life will never be achieved by anything less than ... negating oneself and recognizing the meaning of one's life in service to others.

In the midst of all this activity Tolstoy suffered a new form of difficulty with his wife. After the death of Ivan, Sonya took consolation in music, which led to her one-sided affair with the composer and pianist S. I. Taneyev. Feeling misunderstood and unappreciated by her husband, whom others considered a sage, she poured her feeling for devotion into a suffocating pursuit of the reserved musician. Tolstoy's capacity for intense emotion was sorely tried by an inner struggle between his compassion for her and his disappointment and his resentment against the feelings of jealousy. They never faced each other on the "affair." Within a few years' time — and after many rebuffs by Taneyev — Sonya's interest in him slowly died.

In the last month of the last year of the nineteenth century, Tolstoy completed the novel *Resurrection.* Having made this one exception with respect to accepting royalties, he was eager for the book to appear and to receive money for it in order to contribute all that it earned to the cause of an oppressed religious sect, the Dukhobors, whom he aided in leaving Russia and settling in Canada.

It was the first full-length novel he had undertaken in twenty years. While its reputation is pale in contrast with *War and Peace* or *Anna Karenina,* it was greeted with warm enthusiasm in 1900 and sold even more widely than his earlier novels in many countries throughout the world. It is based on a true story Tolstoy had heard from a lawyer he knew. A girl without family, brought up on the country estate of two kindly ladies, was seduced by their nephew, who abandoned her. She gave birth to a baby, left it at a foundling home, tried to work at various jobs, was disappointed by other men, and finally ended up a prostitute. Accused of stealing, she was brought to trial. The nephew who originally seduced her was a member of the jury. He was so affected by the injustice of his own past actions that he decided to marry the girl, but shortly after she had served her sentence she died of typhus.

In that thin net of a true "plot" Tolstoy proposed to hold the richness of his seventy years of experience, his attack on the corrupting influence of society, and his belief in the transformation of one's soul by the awakening of a moral consciousness.

Two movements pass back and forth through the novel. One is the awareness of how every noble instinct in youth is abused and destroyed by the influences of cynicism. The other is that the trivial and deluding attitudes most people hold toward the mysteries of life can be overcome only by withdrawing faith from society and placing one's belief in the value of being good. This is infinitely more important than being "fashionable" or "socially accepted." The novel is very much a book with a message.

It ends somewhat the way *Anna Karenina* ended twenty years before. Like Levin, the hero of *Resurrection* undergoes a religious "enlightenment" and proposes to himself the possibility of finding the reality of life in service to others. But the question must be asked — especially in the light of *What Is Art?* — how good is this novel?

The explicit subject matter of the book lies in exposing the hypocrisy of churches and governments which debase human life. Its goal is to evoke feelings of brotherly love and the mutual responsibility of all in contributing to the spiritual perfection of humanity. The artfulness of the form is surely there: in the communication of feelings concerning entirely believable human characters. It is a book full of vivid portraits of princes, lawyers, convicts, peasants, ladies, and fallen women. But something of the mystery of art is lacking. It is, in a word, *obvious*. The crucial difference between *Resurrection* and Tolstoy's greatest novels is that here the reader knows exactly what the author wants him to think and feel. This is not true of *War and Peace* or *Anna Karenina*. They are elusive and suggestive by virtue of the very richness of possibilities offered. It is said of them that they are "life itself" — and we must make what we can of them. But *Resurrection* is not rich in that way, because it is not ambiguous. The contrast between what Tolstoy considers "living" and "dead" is clear. To be "resurrected" is to recognize what is deadly in the world we live in and to "come to life" through the door the author constantly holds open.

Here is a peculiar paradox: the world's greatest novelist had come to the point at which his clarity of thought narrows rather than enhances the effect of his fiction. Whereas the novelist's art — the moving accounts of personal experiences, the use of fables, parables, striking examples — heightens his nonfiction writing, it is not true that his religious and philosophic understanding improves his novelistic art. *Resurrection* is a "sermon" disguised as a novel.

Nevertheless, it is a wonderful disguise. The psychological insights of the character portrayals are brilliant. For example: in the jury box during the trial, the hero Nekhludov, who is in "dread of the disgrace which would befall him if these people knew what he had done was stifling the remorse that struggled in his soul; for, at this stage of the affair, his strongest feeling was fear for himself." And the dramatic pace is maintained by this truth: that fear for oneself, for the loss of status and the loss of pleasures, as the world sees these things, is at war with remorse and the chance of acting out of compassion. Still, the lever which transposes everything inside-out into right-side-out is always at hand. "It is surprising," Tolstoy writes with his all-consuming simplicity, "that the recognition of one's own baseness should be accompanied by a sense of relief, and yet Nekhludov, for all his distress, felt comforted."

12

The "Other Czar"

Early in 1901 the highest council of the Russian Church, along with the approval of the court, acted on a proposal they had had under consideration for three years: they excommunicated Tolstoy. For all its pretense of being a purely religious issue, this act was undertaken for political reasons. It was a joint government and Church effort to deflate Tolstoy's popularity, for the influence he had upon Russian youth by this time was accurately recognized as a direct threat to the stability of the State. In those days it was said that Russia had two Czars — Nicholas II and Tolstoy — and it remained to be seen who was supreme.

The edict of excommunication did indeed cause a sensation but not of the nature hoped for by Tolstoy's opponents. He was, to put it simply, the best-loved citizen in the nation; he was the most powerful champion of the downtrodden; he was the voice of conscience against all forces of oppression. People who swarmed the Moscow streets hailed him. Letters of sympathy or more properly of congratulations poured in for him. Every sort of individual and group, from members of the aristocracy to factory workers, sent greetings, gifts, flowers, telegrams. Students organized protest demonstrations, not because they felt concerned that the Church had formally rejected Tolstoy — when he had long since rejected the Church — but because it was an opportunity to show popular support for the man who had defended them best and encouraged them most.

Sonya was distressed by the excommunication. She was still a communicant of the Orthodox Church, and she saw to it that most of her children remained "believers." But she rose to her husband's defense with outrage and indignation, and published a letter in newspapers both at home and abroad making the point that there are many outside the Church who live more truly Christian lives than certain high ecclesiastics.

The edict of excommunication had exactly the opposite effect from the one intended. It made Tolstoy the rallying point for all hopes of political and social improvement in what remained a police state, a tyrannical despotism. Three weeks after the excommunication was announced (and in the light of new antigovernment demonstrations) Tolstoy wrote an article as "An Appeal to the Czar and His Officials" outlining his proposals for minimal reforms. It was in no sense a utopian document suggesting anything that the government might not sensibly have acted on. It stated the case for popular grievances and appealed for action on four principles: to grant the peasants equal rights with other citizens, to remove all barriers to education, to abolish limitations on religious liberty, and to establish equal treatment under the law. None of the points in this democratic bill of rights was acted upon by the court. Obviously the medieval leaders of Russia, unable to anticipate their being swept to oblivion in 1917-18, were not even able to anticipate the revolt of 1905.

In the spring, the Tolstoys returned to Yasnaya Polyana. Now that their grown-up children were married only their youngest daughter, Alexandra, remained with them. But many of the family visited. Masha at that time first became involved with a problem destined to grow over the years into such proportions that it finally burst apart the ties binding Tolstoy and his wife to each other. This was the issue of Tolstoy's will.

Tolstoy wanted to make certain that after his death not only Sonya but Chertkov as well would be executors of all his writings, that he should under no condition be buried with the rites of the church, and that his heirs should make no attempt to profit from his literary works. He asked Masha to arrange for these stipulations to be added to his will and to keep it secret. By accident, Sonya

Tolstoy and family in the garden at Yasnaya Polyana.

found out about it. Her inexhaustible anger and persistent opposition eventually wore Tolstoy down, and this version of the will was destroyed. But the battle over the issues had just begun.

In the summer, malaria as well as other illnesses attacked Tolstoy, and by September it was decided that, as he could not be expected to survive another winter in the north, he should be moved to a warmer climate. A wealthy countess in St. Petersburg offered the Tolstoy family the use of her estate near Yalta, on the southern shore of the Crimea. The train trip was arduous for the seventy-three-year-old man; all along the route south, and especially in the cities of Kharkov and Sevastopol, throngs greeted his arrival with the warm popular ovations of well-wishers for "the other czar."

Although Tolstoy came close to death a number of times, although he suffered a heart attack, typhoid fever, inflammation of the lungs, complicated by rheumatism and liver complaints, and although the period of convalescence lasted for nearly two years, the physical constitution of the man who as a youth had once hoped to be "the strongest man in the world" enabled him to recover. One ironic plot was foiled during this period. The Church attempted to keep a priest close at hand to announce that Tolstoy had recanted and had died in the arms of the Church — whether it was true or not. But this "danger" was swiftly eliminated.

Tolstoy wrote — despite all — both essays and letters,

including his final letters of advice to the Czar. When it became clear that the government would take no action whatsoever, Tolstoy offered the letters for publication with these comments:

Every thinking person of our time cannot fail to see that there are only two ways out of the oppressive and menacing situation with which we are now confronted: one, though very difficult, is bloody revolution; the second is recognition by the governments of their obligation not to oppose the law of progress, not to defend the old or, as we have done, return to the past, but rather to understand the direction in which humanity is moving and to lead the people in that direction.

Inasmuch as the Russian government had rejected the latter possibility, Tolstoy could only appeal to the people to minimize the catastrophe of "bloody revolution."

When the life of people is unmoral [he wrote in his diary at this time] and their relations are not based on love, but on egoism, then all technical improvements, the increase of man's power over nature, steam, electricity, the telegraph, every machine, gunpowder, and dynamite produce the impression of dangerous toys placed in the hands of children.

The revolt was close at hand. By January 1904, shortly after Tolstoy was well enough to return to his home, the Russo-Japanese War began. Here was only one more instance of the hypocrisy and insanity of governments:

two nations, both professing national religions that forbid killing, had ordered their peoples to murder each other — for what? For delusions such as "national honor, or materialistic advantages such as economic control of a tail of land. It was the people who would suffer while the fat grew fatter. But not only were there the ignorant who thought they would suffer more if they refused to serve in the army; even worse was the fact that the enlightened, the educated, actually volunteered. To his personal sorrow Tolstoy's own son Andrei was one of them.

For all he had written against war in the past, Tolstoy found it necessary to write more. However, the situation was too far gone. The unpopular and disastrous war, steadily heading toward defeat for the Russians, let loose the pent-up frustrations of the people. Riots broke out; soldiers deserted; there were peasant uprisings and student demonstrations. A member of the Czar's cabinet was assassinated. An organization of workers marching to the Winter Palace in St. Petersburg was ruthlessly shot down. That particular massacre brought about the alliance of all the working-class parties and led to their becoming the decisive force in bringing about some degree of the hoped-for change.

The government made a modest concession: it called for a national congress to "advise" it. This inadequate proposal resulted in a general strike. The leaders of the two major groups in the working-class movement, Lenin and Trotsky, operating out of St. Petersburg, attempted to establish similar organizations throughout the country. In the meanwhile, the government announced its new concessions: giving the national congress legislative powers, guaranteeing fundamental civil liberties and a democratic vote. These, and various techniques of division and distraction, split the unity and stemmed the force of the revolutionary movement. It was not until the First World War erupted that the opportunity presented itself again — but during the intervening twelve years Lenin and Trotsky (each in his own way) laid the foundations — for the ultimate destruction of Czarist autocracy.

Tolstoy did not support the hope that a representative constitutional government for Russia would make matters much better. He maintained that to abolish the economic bases for oppression and inequality the peasants must control the land they work. In this respect he was prophetic for, twelve years later, the Communist revolution swept to success under the slogan of "All land to the peasants!"

But Tolstoy himself had lost his position as spokesman for the Russian people. The lesson of the 1905 revolt was that those in command (who imagine they have a monopoly of violence in the State) respond only to violence. For the Russians, the approach of civil disobedience, nonviolent resistance to evil, had proved unsuccessful. The heart had gone out of their devotion to Tolstoy; it went over to the "bloody" revolutionists.

Constantly aware of the imminence of death, Tolstoy

no longer planned large writing schemes or even many more short works. He labored on an anthology of readings similar to a volume of selections he had edited earlier called *Thoughts of Wise People for Every Day.* This new *Circle of Reading* likewise consisted of passages from Greek, Roman, Oriental, and European sources, as well as selections from Tolstoy's own writings. All of it reflects his concern for a spiritual life and the approaches to it — totally regardless of the perversions of separate "churches" which have pretentiously arrogated to themselves the absurdity of being exclusively "right."

His family life had become so steadily hardened in its patterns of dispute and dissatisfaction that, in one clash with two of his sons, he revealed that fact that "I pack my suitcase every week!" The thought of escape from the trap in which he remained had never left him. The opposition not only to his ideas but to his way of life, the pressure of his family's greed (as he saw it), and the emptiness of their lives tortured him. But then Masha's death and a particularly delicate surgical operation which Sonya survived were followed by a peaceful breathing space for which both were grateful.

The political situation had not truly improved. The national congresses were convened and dissolved by the Czar and, through his supporters, came to be dominated by the most conservative party. Wherever and whenever any demonstration of public protest was expressed, the government responded with ruthless measures. Execution became the order of the day. And in reaction — terrorists assassinated, thieves robbed, estates were burned to the ground. (One of Sonya's brothers was murdered during the course of a strike.) The feeling of living in a prison became more prevalent than ever.

Tolstoy wrote another series of articles between 1906 and 1907 appealing to the Russian people not only to abjure violence but to recognize that industrialization itself is a curse, urging them to devote themselves to the simplicity and self-sufficiency of an agricultural life. But it was all too late. The lures of "the easy life" coupled with the justifiable loathing for the reactionary regime had determined the people's choice: for revolution and industrialization. Russia was determined to go the way of the West.

Tolstoy devoted himself again to teaching children and wrote various tales and parables, pamphlets, and even an account called *The Teaching of Christ Told for Children.*

After 1905 many of Tolstoy's closest followers — including Chertkov — were allowed to return to Russia from exile. And, while that cheered him, it created further problems in its own way.

13

Eighty Years Old

Early in the summer of 1908 Chertkov bought property adjacent to Yasnaya Polyana and built a large manor house. From there he visited with The Master nearly every day. He treated Tolstoy as a saint. He hung on his every word, even when he sanctimoniously tried to improve upon them. He arranged for photographers to record him in pictures. He managed the foreign publications of Tolstoy's writings prohibited in Russia. And he pursued a policy of preserving every scrap that The Master wrote — including copies of letters and diary entries — in the archives he organized and called "the Vault." To her ever-increasing misery, Sonya saw Chertkov leave the house after each visit with a small bag bulging with manuscripts. The fear that Chertkov was in possession of

ф.58. Л. Н. Толстой.

Tolstoy at about age eighty at Yasnaya Polyana.

material which he would publish after Tolstoy's death, for his own advantage rather than for the benefit of the family, drove her nearly out of her mind. Perhaps most gruesome of all is the fact that Chertkov sat there with a notebook in hand, taking down their remarks while Sonya and Tolstoy argued over these very points.

Tolstoy believed that the private ownership of property is the root of social evil — the crucial condition separating people and making them hostile to each other. Sonya, on the other hand, remained absolutely insistent upon her property rights in total disregard of his feelings. It was all well and good for him to preach brotherhood and selflessness and vegetarianism, she thought, but it was she who had to arrange for two different sets of meals every day, it was she who suffered when the management of the estate went poorly, she to whom their sons appealed for loans of money. Tolstoy might be admired for advocating communal use of natural resources; she was made out to be an ogre for calling the police when peasants fished in her pond or stole trees from her woods. Granting her investment in maintaining the traditional way of life with which she was identified, it is understandable that she could only consider it the derangement of an unbalanced mind for Tolstoy to imagine they ought to give away their property to the peasants and live among them as equals. (It is an everlasting irony that, after Tolstoy's death, and with the success of the Communist revolution, that was precisely Sonya's fate.)

Tolstoy was reproached by both followers and critics for living as he did. Was he naïve or a hypocrite to remain "in the lap of luxury" (as they imagined it), consoled merely by the legal trick of having turned his property over to his wife? Tolstoy's explanation to himself was that his religious beliefs did not free him of his duty to his wife. If he abandoned her in order to live a life more in keeping with his ideals, would he not be feeding his own vanity, for he would have placed his selfish desires above his responsibility to others. "If I wish to lessen my sins," he wrote to one of his followers, "I shall try to lessen them in my present existence, for I can on no account change my situation without committing new sins now." There was always the hope that he might persuade Sonya to his way of thinking. This abnormal situation, permanently filled with conflict, perpetuated his suffering. Things did not get better; they were either more or less miserable.

In the public world, the political position of the country had become so unbearable under the oppressive actions of the government that Tolstoy burst forth with a flaming denunciation. *I Cannot Be Silent* it is called, and it was taken to heart throughout the world, not only in Russia, as the most articulate expression of all who felt misused by tyrannical power. In his most vivid style, Tolstoy describes the executions taking place. The government defends its policies by the pretense that it is protecting its citizens. In that case, Tolstoy pleads, put me in jail, too, or better still execute me, because I refuse to accept being protected and defended against my fellow citizens in this way. I will not give even tacit sanction to such actions, allowing the government to think it is doing me a favor by killing my fellow men.

In all honesty Tolstoy imagined that this declaration would result in his imprisonment. But the government had no intention of making itself the object of national and international outrage by martyring the world's foremost writer. Instead, it took measures against his followers. Chertkov was ordered to leave the house he had built and move close to Moscow. Tolstoy's secretary was arrested (on the charge of distributing "revolutionary literature") and taken away by the police literally from the family's presence.

At the very time when a committee approached him with plans for a national celebration of his eightieth birthday, Tolstoy was so distressed by his own life that he had begun to keep a secret diary — in a home where there had been no secrets and where one's diary was available to the other. Tolstoy rejected all the proposals suggested for a Tolstoy Jubilee or grandiose holiday on the occasion of his birthday. His wishes were respected. But at the end of August, while the family alone gathered to honor him — his wife, children, and grandchildren — messages of congratulation began to pour in. From all over the world some two thousand telegrams arrived.

They came from people in all walks of life: from humble laborers to royalty; from distinguished public figures to convicts in prison. A message of praise signed by hundreds of Englishmen including Thomas Hardy, H. G. Wells, and Bernard Shaw was delivered. From the United States and from Australia the greetings came. There were messages to this pacifist from fellow survivors of his Sevastopol days; and from students of the University of Kazan, from which he did not graduate.

The gifts that poured in included cigarettes, which he did not smoke, and wine, which he did not drink. Despite his recognition of "so much insincerity and falseness," Tolstoy was moved by certain expressions. He said:

One thing is pleasant: in nearly all these letters, congratulations, and addresses, the same thing is repeated — it has simply become a truism — that I have destroyed religious delusions and opened the way for the search after truth. If it is true, it is just what I have wanted and tried to do all my life, and this is very dear to me.

While he may have taken some gratification in believing his public life had been successful, his private life went from bad to worse. In his secret diary again and again he writes that he *wants to leave.* The moral problem as he put it was this: "If I go, do I do it for myself? In remaining, I know that I do not do it for myself."

Sonya's maddening behavior is exemplified in an inci-

The last photograph of Tolstoy, shown here with his wife. The photograph was taken six weeks before his death.

dent the following summer. An International Congress for Peace to be held at Stockholm invited Tolstoy to give an address. He accepted and drafted a speech. Sonya became hysterical; accused him of wanting to go away for good; insisted that he was too old, that his health was too poor, that, at least, he could not go without her. He agreed that she should accompany him. Sonya prepared a new wardrobe and looked forward to the "excursion." Drawbacks to the whole undertaking became so oppressive to Tolstoy that he decided not to attend. Sonya then insisted that she should go in his place. Only the fact that the Congress was postponed settled the matter.

But the primary issue of rights to Tolstoy's writings continued to lie between them like an exposed sword. He wanted above all to make certain that his books would become public property. In September of 1909, along with his daughter Alexandra and Dr. Makovitski (his physician at Yasnaya Polyana), Tolstoy set off to visit Chertkov. In the course of that stay a will was drawn up making all of Tolstoy's published and unpublished works written after 1881 freely accessible to all who wished to use them. Chertkov was designated executor of the will. It was signed and witnessed. Tolstoy left in the belief that his intentions were now protected by a legal instrument.

Fortunately, Alexandra had the foresight to show the document to a lawyer in Moscow in order to verify the legality of these provisions. It turned out that the will would not hold up in court because the law prohibited bequeathing property to "nobody"; a specific person would have to be designated. The trip back proved exhausting and Tolstoy had a relapse. While the doctor and Alexandra worked feverishly to revive him, Sonya hovered over Tolstoy, begging him to tell her where the keys were to his writing desk.

Recovery came slowly, and the problem of the will continued to plague him. In the end, it was settled by his determining to make Alexandra sole heir. He had confidence that she would carry out his wishes. In the final version of the will even the works written prior to 1881 were included in the bequest. It would be Alexandra's responsibility to take care of her mother. The will was executed in secrecy from Sonya; but the tone of conspiracy which communicated itself fed her worst fears, and she acted on the intuition that something fearful was being plotted against her. After forty-seven years of married life they had been brought to this.

Tolstoy repeatedly expressed his admiration for the Buddhist practice of abandoning all worldly goods in old age and wandering as a beggar — already separated from the things of this life — awaiting death. Sonya frequently threatened suicide. After a heated argument she would rush out of the house and hide in a ditch until Tolstoy fetched her back. During his next brief visit to Chertkov, she simulated illness in order to make him return. When he did not come immediately, she attempted to poison herself. She saw Tolstoy happy in the company of his followers and gloomy when he was alone with her. In her view, Chertkov stood as the chief obstacle between them. Most of all he represented the idea that Tolstoy's writings were being "withdrawn" *from her.* In hysterical frenzies — including further attempts at suicide and feigned attempts — she tortured herself and her husband. Their children acted between them, either trying to reconcile them or taking sides. The misery they caused each other had no remedy. But the end was near.

14

Escape

In the middle of the night, in the first hours of October 28, 1910, Tolstoy packed a bag and stealthily escaped from Yasnaya Polyana. Overcome by the futility of all his effort to make peace with Sonya, he could remain with her no longer. It had become impossible for him to work. For her sake he had agreed not to see Chertkov again, but she gave him no rest. She spied on his every movement, following him in a carriage if he went out riding, watching him through opera glasses, eavesdropping behind doors, waking him in the middle of the night — either to beg his forgiveness or to demand access to his papers. When he was confined to bed with illness, she removed his writings from his study to her own room. Suspicious of everything, she looked everywhere for proof.

And then she found it. Concealed in one of his boots, Tolstoy had misplaced a volume of his secret diaries. Sonya discovered in reading it, not only reflections on the family situation but enough references to the final will to inflame her fears even further. Her hysteria knew no limits. His resistence could no longer endure. During the evening of October 27th he listened to her rummaging in his study looking for the will, for letters from Chertkov, for other volumes of his secret diary. He could bear it no longer. When she was asleep he cautiously packed a few things to take with him, wrote her a letter, and then called Alexandra and Dr. Makovitski. The horses were quietly readied, and Tolstoy set off (accompanied by the doctor) to the nearest railroad station.

He had remained out of habit, out of duty, and out of love for her — until the moment when he not only saw the degree of the offense against himself but considered the possibility as well that only by his leaving might she have a chance to recover.

In the letter he left behind he thanks her, he tries to offer consolation to her, and he gives her no hope of ever seeing him again. "I am doing," he wrote, "what old men of my age commonly do: leaving this worldly life in order to live out my last days in peace and solitude." Before she had finished reading the letter, Sonya rushed out raving and tried to drown herself in the pond. Dragged back to the house by Alexandra and servants, she tried to throw herself out of a window. All objects with which

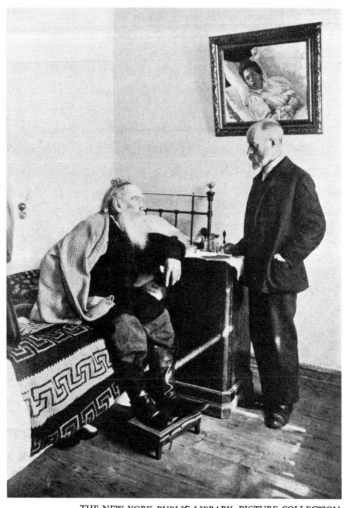

The last illness. Tolstoy in his bedroom talking to Dr. Makovitski.

she might fatally wound herself were taken away from her, and she was kept under constant observation. The other children were summoned; doctors were called in. What Sonya had lived in dread of — for one reason or another — throughout the forty-eight years of her marriage had finally happened. Her husband, the genius in whose glory she had basked, the lover whose children she had borne, the sage whose unworldliness she had contested, had finally abandoned her.

The eighty-two-year-old man, who had dreamed of turning his back on civilization and living like a peasant, sat in a third-class railroad coach. After long silence he turned to the faithful doctor accompanying him and said, "I wonder how Sonya is now. I'm sorry for her." But then, "How fine it is to be free!" It took more than six hours to travel seventy miles away from Yasnaya Polyana, during which time the police, informed of his departure, were already on the lookout for him. The flight of the man who wished to abandon the world and live out his last days in "peace and solitude" was being described in newspaper headlines, as much of a national event as if the Czar had chosen to abdicate.

Tolstoy spent the afternoon and night at the Optina Monastery on his way to visit his sister, who was a nun at the Shamardino Convent. He informed Alexandra of his whereabouts by wire. The next morning one of Chertkov's assistants arrived with news. In the afternoon he visited with his sister. He considered the possibility of renting a hut in the neighborhood and actually looked for one. The following morning Alexandra arrived, although he had not asked her to come, bringing the fearful information that Sonya had guessed where he was and intended to come after him. Tolstoy immediately decided to move on. Over maps and train schedules in his room at the inn they tried to make a plan. But with only a vague intention to go south first, they left the question open and tried to sleep. At four in the morning he awoke the doctor and Alexandra, having been terrified by the thought that Sonya might arrive before they had left, and feeling that they must be off at once.

On board the train it was obvious that there was a police agent among the curious who kept watching the three of them. Early in the afternoon Tolstoy suffered a chill; Dr. Makovitski discovered he was running a fever. At the next train stop, Astapovo, the doctor arranged to have Tolstoy provided with a bed in the station master's house. It became clear that he was severely ill, but in the morning he seemed better. Alexandra asked if he wished to inform the family, but he requested to see only Chertkov — who came as quickly as possible. That evening Tolstoy's oldest son Sergei arrived. A specialist was called from Moscow. Gradually a crew of policemen and a battalion of newspaper reporters gathered at the tiny train station. Late during the night Sonya arrived in a special train along with her children, a doctor, and a nurse, But in a council of all the doctors and Tolstoy's children it was decided to keep her from seeing him.

During the course of the remaining few days Tolstoy struggled hard to continue dictating letters, notes, entries for his diary; but the pneumonia had progressed so that he often fell into unconsciousness or spoke only in fragments, as in a delirium. "To seek, always to seek . . ." he whispered to Alexandra. "On Sonya," he said, "much is falling. We have arranged badly." "To escape . . . I must escape!" And "Truth . . . I love much."

At midnight on November 7th, Tolstoy, asleep, was failing rapidly. It was agreed to allow Sonya to enter the room. She kissed her husband's forehead, sank to her knees, and whispered: "Forgive me!" At a quarter to six in the morning Tolstoy died.

He had written in a private letter once:

It is generally supposed that there is something mystical in our view of life and death. But there is nothing of the kind.

I like my garden. I like reading a book. I like caressing a child. By dying I lose all this, and therefore I do not wish to die, and I fear death.

It may be that my whole life consists of such temporary desires and their gratification. If so I cannot help being afraid of what will end these desires. But if these desires and their gratification have given

The house in which Tolstoy died.

way and been replaced in me by another desire —
the desire to do the will of God, to give myself to
Him in my present state and in any possible future
state — then the more my desires have changed the
less I fear death, and the less does death exist for
me. And if my desires be completely transformed,
then nothing but life remains and there is no death.
To replace what is earthly and temporary by what
is eternal is the way of life, and along it we must
travel. But in what state his own soul is — each one
knows for himself.

Sergei Tolstoy gives the following account of what
happened once his father was dead:

"The doors of the house were open and a thousand
people came to pay Tolstoy their last respects.

"Mother sat all day at the head of the bed, her head
shaking. It was painful to watch her. The painter Paster-
nak made a drawing of him, the sculptor Merkurov made
a cast. Photographers were busy and someone drew the
outline of his shadow on the wall. I was asked if his skull
could be opened, but after consultation with the family
we refused it, knowing how Father hated scientific ex-
periments of that kind. . . .

"On November 8th we four brothers carried the coffin
out of the house and into the train, decorated with fir-tree
branches and wreathes. The whole family went in another carriage and in a third one the newspaper corre-
spondents. We arrived at seven A.M. at Yasnaya, by

which time we had already been inundated with telegrams of sympathy. A great crowd had assembled at the
station. We carried the coffin out again, and then the
peasants of Yasnaya took our places and the funeral procession, with funeral songs, moved along the road which
Father had so often taken. It was a still, misty day; snow
lay here and there, and there was a slight frost. I think
the crowd numbered from three to four thousand people.
As we moved along I was told that Chertkov had arranged that the coffin should not be brought into the
house and that it should be left unopened but for a
few moments halt in front of the entrance. I protested
against that and so did Mother and my brothers, knowing
that many people would like to see Father once more. I
hurried ahead. Our old servant and I pulled out the frame
of the door that led into Father's favorite study, and there
we put the coffin. The procession by the coffin went on
from 11 A.M. to 2:30 P.M. . . . Finally the coffin was
closed.

"He was buried, as he had wanted, in the place in the
woods which he had indicated. Everybody knelt down,
only a solitary policeman remained on his feet. Someone
shouted: 'On your knees, policeman!'

"There were no speeches at the graveside. My mother
was silent and controlled. I hoped she would cry, but she
did not shed a tear. Chertkov was not there.

"A dark autumn night set in and gradually everybody
drifted away.

"Tolstoy's burial was the first public burial without a church service, which is what he wanted. . . .

"Mother fell ill and had to keep to her bed for about a fortnight. Her sister came to try to console her. She was crushed with grief, but no longer mentioned suicide. Gradually, she began to return to her usual occupations — correcting proof, busying herself in the house, etc. But her state of mind was desperate. . . ."

Sonya's two-sentence diary entry for December 11th reads as follows: "Have put away my husband's things, to protect them from moths. How terrible life can be."

It had been Tolstoy's belief that, if man understood better the nature of existence, life would not be terrible. At the time of his excommunication from the Church, he wrote:

I believe in God, whom I understand as Spirit, as love, as the Source of all. I believe that He is in me and I in Him. I believe that the will of God is most clearly and intelligently expressed in the teaching of the man Jesus, whom to consider as God and pray to, I esteem the greatest blasphemy. I believe that man's true welfare lies in fulfilling God's will, and His will is that men should love one another and should consequently do to others as they wish others to do to them — of which it is said in the Gospels that in this is the law and the prophets. I believe therefore that the meaning of life of every man is to be found only in increasing the love that is in him; that this increase of love leads man, even in this life, to ever greater and greater blessedness, and after death gives him the more blessedness the more love he has, and helps more than anything else towards the establishment of the Kingdom of God on earth: that is, to the establishment of an order of life in which the discord, deception and violence that now rule will be replaced by free accord, by truth, and by the brotherly love of one for another.

All his life long Tolstoy knew that an idea is only as good as the actions that express it. He tried to act according to his beliefs.

The last portrait of Tolstoy.

Suggested Reading List

A Selected Bibliography
of Works by and about Tolstoy

Nikolenka's Childhood. Introduced by Ernest J. Simmons. New York. Pantheon Books.

Leo Tolstoy's Short Stories. Volume One. Edited and Introduced by Ernest J. Simmons. New York. The Modern Library.

Contains: A History of Yesterday. The Raid. A Billiard-Maker's Notes. The Wood-Felling. Sevastopol in December 1854. Sevastopol in May 1855. Sevastopol in August 1855. Meeting a Moscow Acquaintance in the Detachment. The Snow Storm. Lucerne. Albert. Three Deaths. Strider: The Story of a Horse. The Porcelain Doll.

Leo Tolstoy's Short Stories. Volume Two. Edited and Introduced by Ernest J. Simmons. New York. The Modern Library.

Contains: God Sees the Truth but Waits. A Prisoner in the Caucasus. The Bear-Hunt. What Men Live By. A Spark Neglected Burns the House. Two Old Men. Where Love Is God Is. Evil Allures but Good Endures. Little Girls Wiser than Men. Elias. The Story of Ivan the Fool. The Repentant Sinner. The Three Hermits. The Imp and the Crust. How Much Land Does a Man Need? A Grain as Big as a Hen's Egg. The Godson. The Empty Drum. Esarhaddon, King of Assyria. Work, Death and Sickness. Three Questions. The Memoirs of a Madman. After the Ball. Fedor Kuzmich. Alyosha.

Leo Tolstoy's Short Novels. Volume One. Edited and Introduced by Ernest J. Simmons. New York. The Modern Library.

Contains: Two Hussars. A Landlord's Morning. Family Happiness. Polikushka. The Cossacks.

Leo Tolstoy's Short Novels. Volume Two. Edited and Introduced by Ernest J. Simmons. New York. The Modern Library.

Contains: The Death of Ivan Ilyich. The Devil. The Kreutzer Sonata. A Talk among Leisured People. Walk in the Light while There Is Light.

Master and Man. Father Sergius. Hadji Murad. The Forged Coupon.

Leo Tolstoy's Selected Essays. Edited and Introduced by Ernest J. Simmons. New York. The Modern Library.

Contains: Preface to *The Christian Teaching.* Religion and Morality. Reason and Religion. A Reply to the Synod's Edict of Excommunication. What Is Religion and Wherein Lies Its Essence? Christianity and Patriotism. Partriotism and Government. Address to the Swedish Peace Congress in 1909. Why Do Men Stupefy Themselves? The First Step. Conclusion: *The Kingdom of God Is Within You.* "Thou Shalt Not Kill." What's To Be Done. I Cannot Be Silent.

War and Peace. Translated by Constance Garnett. New York. The Modern Library.

Anna Karenina. Translated by Constance Garnett. Edited and Introduced by Leonard J. Kent and Nina Berberova. New York. The Modern Library.

A Confession, The Gospel in Brief, and *What I Believe.* Translated and Introduced by Aylmer Maude. New York. Oxford University Press (The World's Classics).

Russian Stories and Legends. New York. Pantheon Books.

What Is Art? and *Essays on Art.* Translated and Introduced by Aylmer Maude. New York. Oxford University

Press (The World's Classics).

Resurrection. Translated by Vera Traill. Foreword by Alan Hodge. New York. The New American Library (A Signet Classic).

The Kingdom of God Is Within You. Translated by Leo Wiener. Introduction by Kenneth Rexroth. New York. Noonday Press.

Last Diaries. Translated by Lydia Weston-Kesich. Edited and Introduced by Leon Stilman. New York. G. P. Putnam's Sons (A Capricorn Book).

Leo Tolstoy. Volume One and Volume Two by Ernest J. Simmons. New York. Random House (A Vintage Book). This is the most outstanding biographical study of Tolstoy — as distinguished for its wisdom as it is for its scholarship.